P. C. Jones

CW00525592

James,
Best wishes
[signature]
4.7.08

But Headmaster!

But Headmaster!

EPISODES FROM THE LIFE OF AN
INDEPENDENT SCHOOL HEADMASTER

IAN BEER

GREENBANK PRESS

Published by Greenbank Press
Greenbank, East Horrington, Wells, Somerset BA5 3DR

© Ian Beer 2001

British Library Cataloguing in Publication Data
A catalogue record for this book is available from the British Library

ISBN 0 9523699 7 4

Designed by Bob Elliott
Typeset by Hope Services (Abingdon) Ltd.
Printed by MPG Books Ltd, Bodmin, Cornwall

CONTENTS

HEAD MASTER, HARROW SCHOOL · 1981–1991

MARLBOROUGH COLLEGE · 1955–1961
AND MISCELLANEOUS MATTERS

PREFACE

IF it had not been for dinner parties, this small book would not have been written. Too often, on the way home from a dinner, I recalled other guests saying 'you really must write-down all these memories' or 'and when will the book be published?' I did not set out to write an autobiography although, as it has turned out, the reminiscences in this book add up to a lot of my life.

An autobiography would have mentioned and and thanked many to whom I owe so much but whose names are not to be found in this book. They include: D. B. Jones, E. A. G. Marlar, Jack Cummings, Dr Sidney Smith, The Reverend Hartley Bird, Dr Windsor Lewis, Kenneth Keast, Basil Handford, Raymond Venables, Michael Pailthorpe, Andrew Bishop and Sir John Akehurst. All these and many others influenced and helped me over the course of my professional life.

There is also a whole category of people not directly referred to in this book who are the mainstay of any boarding school and must never be forgotten. They are the non-teaching staff—the matrons, the nurses, the cooks, the cleaners, the works department staff who maintain the school, the groundsman, the gardeners and so many others. At Harrow there were three members of the non-teaching staff for every teacher appointed. To all of them in every school I served I say thank you. Considerations of space only allow me to name a few.

At Ellesmere: Sgt Page, Matron Bates, Mr Tom Edwards the painter, Mr Joe Edwards the carpenter, Ruby and Bernie of the laundry, Christine, Doreen, Llinos and Mrs Jones who helped in the house and with the children.

At Lancing: Mr Deacon, who taught our children and countless others to swim, Mr Spurdle the caterer, Mr Laming the Verger and Mrs Laming the Head Master's wife's help.

At Harrow: Mr Peter Sharples the Estates Bursar, Mr Graham Palmer of the works department, Mr Wilkinson, Custos, and Mr Arnold, Custos, Mr Holdaway the head gardener, and Mr Tom Loftus of the farm.

However it is Herbert, the Head Master's butler at Harrow, who is representative of so many of the non-teaching staff in all the schools. He joined the staff as a very young lad in the 1920s and served as houseboy, houseman, and Head Master's butler when Dr James was leading Harrow in the days when each House had many servants. When my predecessor Michael Hoban succeeded Dr James there were about twelve on the staff working in the Head Master's boarding house, amongst their number Herbert who also looked after Sir Winston Churchill whenever he visited Harrow, something he was extremely proud of. By the time Michael Hoban retired there was only a part-time daily to help the Head Master's wife and Herbert had been transferred to the central dining hall. He was still allowed to buttle for the Head Master at parties and it was in that capacity that we got to know him. A wonderful loyal servant; he gave his entire life to the school and the school was his life.

One day he became seriously ill and we visited him in Northwick Park hospital. He insisted on giving me one of the few precious items he possessed. Before the 1939–1945 war, when he was a young houseman in the Head Master's house, a sixth former who was leaving had given Herbert a pair of enamelled gold cufflinks to say thank you for looking after him so well whilst he had been at school. Herbert had worn these valuable items once a year only—at Lords for the Eton/Harrow cricket match—and he now wanted me to have them. I was overwhelmed and thinking quickly said that I would be privileged to receive them only on condition that they were to be the property of the Head Master and not me personally. I would see that they were handed down from one Head Master to the next and each Head Master would wear them at the Eton/Harrow cricket match as he had done. He was delighted with the plan; he died the next day.

I decided to telephone the Old Harrovian who had given Herbert the cufflinks although I had never met him. I found out that he lived in the North of Scotland and I spoke to his wife only to learn that her husband had died two days previously, almost at the same time as Herbert.

I want to thank Richard Shymansky, the Harrow photographer, who now has a studio at Eton, for giving permission to print many of his pictures and David Nicholls, a Worthing photographer, who took the picture for the front cover, but whom I have failed to trace.

Especially though I thank Richard Hudson, my publisher, for his enthusiasm in accepting the script for publication, for his diligence in advising and editing, and for his friendship and encouragement at a time when I began to think it might be best not to publish at all. I might have been a confident headmaster but an author is a different matter, as many of my erstwhile senior colleagues understand having edited some of my speeches in the past. I am also indebted once again to my wife, Angela, my brother Stafford and his partner Allenna, our three children and their spouses and my sister-in-law, Susie Bromley, for reading the script and making invaluable comments, all of which I acted upon.

Lastly I thank you, the reader, for being interested enough to turn the pages. I hope you will enjoy the book and have a laugh every now and again as I did nearly every day of my working life.

IAN BEER

London
September 2001

꧁꧂

WHILST I have been writing this book I have realised more and more what a fantastic support my wife, Angela, has been. There is hardly a page where she is not involved in some capacity or other: entertaining all the visitors; quietly supporting individual pupils needing help; dealing with enquiries from parents thinking of sending their child to the school; listening to the worries of parents who already have; watching endless team games on the touchline and school and house plays; playing cello in the orchestra; teaching history and french; chairing committees of ladies to organise charitable fundraising events; and so much besides. Every member of the community in which she worked knew that her husband could hire or fire, so true friendships were not easy until we left the school, and then we were not supposed to return! At the same time, to prevent isolation, much work was done in the local community and that role often fell on her. To my knowledge, no book has ever been written on the role of a boarding school headmaster's wife; but such a book would make interesting and agonising reading. Her own compilation, published to raise money for The Church of England Children's Society, entitled *Playing Second Fiddle*, is the only reading that gets anywhere near the heart of the matter.

And yet her finest achievement during these thirty years was to give birth to our three wonderful children and to guide them through childhood, adolescence, school and university to three very happy marriages with their own children, while for much of this time time the Headmaster was looking after other people's children.

A FOOTNOTE

The men who have led the old public schools of the United Kingdom have, through their Royal Charters, their Statutes and their custom been given different titles. Not all are headmasters; for example, Marlborough College is led by The Master, Manchester Grammar School by The High Master, George Watson's in Edinburgh by The Principal, Radley by The Warden and so on. I was, therefore, The Headmaster of Ellesmere College but The Head Master of Lancing College and The Head Master of Harrow School.

HEADMASTER
ELLESMERE COLLEGE
1961 – 1969

❧❦❧❦

1

How it all began

'Excuse me, but are you Colonel Story?'

'Yes, I am. Who are you?'

'My name is Ian Beer and I have come to be interviewed for the headship of Ellesmere College.'

He looked me up and down as if I was a soldier newly recruited and on parade. 'You can't be,' he said. 'You are far too young to be a Head Master' and turned as if to go. Very anxiously I had to confirm my presence. 'Sir', I insisted, 'I am here to be interviewed; I have been invited.' His moustache bristled and, sighing, he said 'Well, I suppose you must be correct. Meet me for a drink before dinner.'

All this took place in a Birmingham Hotel one Thursday in March 1961. The hotel, now no longer, is just part of the Bull Ring. Angela, my wife of under three months, and I had been summoned by the Fellows (Governors) of the Midland Division of the Woodard Corporation to attend an interview for the Headship of Ellesmere College which was to become vacant the following September. We had not applied for the job; we had never visited Ellesmere College. I had served Marlborough College for five and a half years and was attracted to starting out married life together in a new environment with, maybe, a pleasant headmaster's house rather than the housemaster's flat in which we had been living for the previous few weeks. We were also curious. We were given only a few days' warning before the interview and I eventually found that I was an extra to the shortlist of six, making seven of us in all.

We had arrived at the hotel at about six o'clock in the evening as requested and it was on arrival that I looked for the Divisional Bursar, Colonel Story, and the above conversation took place. We were dispatched to our rooms and invited to join the Colonel for a drink before we dined on our own in the hotel.

Dressing for dinner I discovered to my dismay that I had not packed any collar studs. Now those were the days when a white shirt was *de rigeur* and the stiff white cutaway collar the very thing for smart young men; certainly for one who aspired to become a headmaster. The hotel did not have a corridor of smart shops as you would find today, but it did have a very smart and imposing ex-Sergeant Major as the hall porter. In some trepidation I sought him out and asked whether he could help me. I think he was greatly amused to see his spare pair of collar studs going off to try their luck in their first interview for a headship.

At that time I was still playing first-class rugby for Bath and was fit and in training. On being asked by my formidable Colonel what I wanted to drink I had no hesitation in asking for an orange squash. The effect this request had on the great soldier was traumatic and I see him now as he exploded and proclaimed 'You cannot drink orange squash as a headmaster!' I proved him wrong, but I was clearly not becoming his frontrunner for the job, although we became the greatest of friends over the coming years.

Dinner was a curious affair as the dining room filled up with strange couples eyeing each other warily, all knowing why they were there but not communicating. It became clear later that Angela and I were by far the youngest and many of them had 'done the circuit' before and were experienced interviewees. The whole ghastly selection process meant far more to them than to us. Indeed, in modern idiom we were very 'laid-back' and must have irritated them beyond belief. We eventually retired for the night and after breakfast met each other again in the large drawing-room where all thirteen of us (one candidate was a bachelor) were to sit until lunchtime. We tried to make polite conversation. The men were thinking of their interviews, and the wives were left to make all the running in the conversation. It was an appalling strain as one by one candidates left the room to be interviewed leaving their wives looking even more anxious, either lapsing into complete silence or becoming more and more talkative as the tension rose. I was the last to be interviewed. A group of about twelve men sat round a green baize table and fired questions at me. I recall little of the interview. I could not speak about the College, never having seen it, and my comments were restricted to exposing my ignorance over financial matters and my over-confident view concerning the education of adolescent boys. I desperately wanted an orange squash.

At lunch we were joined by more Governors, as the Woodard Corporation at that time was responsible for ten schools and all the Governors, who were Fellows of the Corporation, were invited to lunch to help decide on any new appointment to any of the schools. It was quite a party. I had the eagle-eyed Colonel watching me from across the table, muttering as he drank his claret and I my squash. My poor wife was asked to sit at the top table where she was clearly being interviewed informally by the Earl of Cavan in the most relaxed and charming way possible. He asked her whether she wanted to be the wife of a headmaster. Not knowing whether she wanted to be one or not, she managed in true diplomatic fashion to avoid the question. He and his wife became very great friends later and enormous allies to us as the years went by.

After lunch, thirty or more Governors retired to the interviewing room and we went downstairs again to the drawing-room. By this time conversation had almost completely ceased; the tension was almost unbearable. One candidate was summoned upstairs by the Colonel, then another and then, to my surprise, it was my turn again. I recall only two questions. They had honed in on my financial inexperience. 'Now, Mr Beer, tell us more about your experience of handling money.' I mumbled something about my current account and, as far as I can recall, dried up. It was only later that I remembered that I had been Bursar of Ottershaw School, the Surrey LEA boarding school, for four months after leaving Cambridge.

On finishing my Post Graduate Certificate of Education at the end of my fourth year at Cambridge I had noticed an advertisement in *The Times* for the position of temporary Bursar at Ottershaw School. The appointment was to begin immediately as the Bursar had gone into hospital. The advertisement said 'No previous experience necessary. Current driving licence essential. Preparedness to partake of sherry with parents helpful, and willingness to play cricket on Sunday for the Common Room an advantage.' Penurious graduates do not hesitate when faced with such temptation and I sent a telegram to the Headmaster. He replied immediately; I was summoned for interview and appointed on the spot. There were four bank accounts; I managed to balance three of them but the fourth was impossible. The auditors arrived and after much investigation informed me that one account could not be balanced and they would have to take the problem to the Headmaster. This they did, and the Headmaster, all six-foot-five of him, rose from his desk and asked them whether they were properly qualified accountants or not. On receiving their affirmative reply he told them very firmly that if they could not balance the books with their qualifications, how could they expect a Bursar with no qualifications to be able to do it? We left his study and they turned to me saying 'Oh dear, another loss for the Surrey County Council to bear.' I never heard another thing, but the experience was to stand me in very good stead later on in my career when there were financial and other problems with Bursars. It is just a pity that I could not recall it when I needed it most during my interview.

The second question the Governors asked was easy. 'Mr Beer, if you had a Chaplain in a school whom you thought had been there for too many years, what would you do?' 'Move him to another post', I replied. It was only later that I realised that the theoretical question had a practical application; and then I found it was not so easy to put my rather glib reply into practice.

I left the interview room in something of a daze and began walking down the long hotel corridor. Suddenly, the Colonel shouted at me from outside the closed door of the interview room. 'Beer! Just one moment.' I turned, thinking I was going to have to answer more questions, but he simply said 'just go downstairs and tell all the others to go home . . . and you can go home, too.' I could not believe my ears, but I was too slow. By the time I was ready to argue he was back in the security of the interview room. Years later, after many traumatic experiences in my first headship, I often wondered whether that request was not the last test to see whether I was the right man to stand the strain of changing Ellesmere College in 1961.

Somewhat shaken I walked slowly down the corridor thinking of the others who were not to be interviewed the second time. They had been so anxious for their futures and depended on the outcome of the proceedings in a way that did not effect me. I went downstairs, expectant faces looked up at me . . . 'I am sorry', I said, 'but I have been asked to request that we all go home now. I have no idea what is going on but we are to go.'

There was a terrible silence. I grasped my wife and fled in total frustration. We packed our bags and left the hotel only to be halted by the hall porter who requested that we pay our bill. In anger I just scrawled over the bill—'to be paid by the Woodard Corporation', while my wife said to me 'Well, now you will certainly not get the job!' I felt at that time I did not want it anyway, but have had very good reasons since to applaud the Woodard Corporation for their generosity and kindness towards me. I never found out what happened on that day in March 1961, but I did learn that all the other candidates were eventually appointed to headships of a variety of schools in this country and abroad.

As we tried to leave for the second time the hall porter reminded me of my debt which, temporarily blinded by my anger, I had forgotten—'But, Sir, my collar studs . . . ?'

The next day, a Saturday, I had finished my teaching and was sitting having an early lunch with my wife in our housemaster's flat at Marlborough when the telephone went. I was about to leave to play rugby for Bath against Neath and nearly left the telephone to my wife to answer but, concerned that the call might be from a parent, I picked up the receiver. It was the Bishop of Shrewsbury asking me if I would go to Ellesmere the following September as Headmaster.

As we had never visited the School, I had to tell him that we could not make any decision until the following week and that we would visit the

College on Monday. We found a school in the most beautiful part of North Shropshire with outstanding views from the Headmaster's house, but with a curious atmosphere within the school itself. The boys seemed to me to be too polite, too deferential, too smart, whilst the Headmaster, The Reverend R. A. Evans-Prosser, appeared to be a remarkable man. We ate with him in the school dining room and he succeeded in finishing his entire meal before we were halfway through our first course. He informed me that the finances of the school were sound, which was correct, and that future entries were assured which was not quite so correct.

The Headmaster's house was totally covered by Virginia creeper and, as it had a flat roof, it gave a very curious impression from the outside. It was light and airy inside although we found that the wiring was only organised to take 110 volts. Before we moved in, the house had to be rewired and we were determined at some stage in the future to have a proper 'bonnet' (roof) built. I was suspicious that the wiring in the Headmaster's house was symptomatic of the problems within the school as a whole, as my predecessor had been appointed Headmaster in 1935 and had remained in post for the next twenty-six years. He had been appointed an assistant master in 1924. It was becoming clear to me that there was much to be changed.

We realised that were we to accept the headmastership of Ellesmere College we would only have two terms together at Marlborough. I went to see the Master of Marlborough and he told me that he thought I would probably take the job but in taking it I should be aware that either I would make my name or it would be the end of my headmastering career. He thought it was a risk, but we took it and never regretted the move as we grew to love Ellesmere and made so many friends. However, the task ahead proved to be extremely exciting.

2

The Drinks Party

DURING May of that same year I telephoned the Bishop of Shrewsbury, the Right Reverend William Parker, and asked him when we would both be invited to some party at Ellesmere when we might meet the entire staff. I was told by the Bishop that there might be difficulties as parties were not known to be held in the school. I explained to the Bishop that it would be very difficult for me to take over the leadership of the Common Room without meeting the staff briefly at some stage during the summer term. He sympathised and promised to telephone after he had talked with the Headmaster but said that he was not optimistic. However, he eventually telephoned back and informed us of the date when a party would be given for us. There was no question of our staying with the Headmaster and so the Bishop was pleased that we were invited to stay with the Divisional Bursar, the redoubtable Colonel 'Storky' Story. To this day I am not aware of his first name; no one ever used it.

The party turned out to be something of a milestone for me. The evening was warm and the view across the North Shropshire plain to the Bredon and the Berwyn Hills was beautiful. The members of the Common Room were charming to us, but I worried about the age of one or two of my senior colleagues, for I learnt that there was no retiring age. That evening I also met for the first time the school doctor who was to become one of our greatest personal friends. I was standing on one of the terraces in our garden talking with one of the masters when a voice behind me whispered, none too quietly, 'Thank God you have arrived. This is the first drink I have ever had in the school.' I turned to face Dr Matt Samson who as well as being doctor to the College had a practice in Overton, near Oswestry. Matt Samson made one or two comments to me, which gave me a hint of the task that lay ahead. It was clear that much had to be done and when I found few books in the school dated after the 1939–1945 war, I realised that the school had almost stood still during those important years from 1949 to 1961.

This occasion was only my second meeting with the Headmaster and turned out to be my last. He was kindness itself and presented me with a book which he told me would help me in running the school. When I got home and studied it I realised that it was a brilliant bursar's manual but had nothing to do with headmastering. As I knew I had to be my own bursar, however, I was grateful to learn a little more of the bursar's trade, supplementing what I had learnt at Ottershaw. There was one amazing entry. The book informed me that I must be aware of the gardeners who were, according to the Headmaster, 'crooks'. On reading further I found that they had requested to work a half an hour longer during the summer months whilst requesting to work for a half an hour less during the winter months. Over the year this would balance out, but it would enable them to tend their own gardens during the winter. The book informed me that it took a little while for the Headmaster to realise they would be cheating the school of five hours work, and pay was suitably deducted. I was totally baffled by this entry and had to ask the Headmaster over the telephone what this meant. He said to me, 'Surely you realise that they took their fortnight's holiday in the summer and therefore would be depriving the school of a half an hour per day throughout that time but don't worry, pay has been deducted.' I began to realise the kind of man I was to follow.

3

⁂

The Black Lion and Corporal Punishment

An idyllic summer term at Marlborough slowly drew to a close and we began to concentrate on our move to Ellesmere. On our return from a holiday in Italy, we followed the furniture van to Ellesmere, although we were initially to live in the Black Lion Hotel, due to the re-wiring of the Headmaster's residence. We had only been married eight months and owned little furniture and few belongings. We set about the salerooms of Shropshire to find furniture for the large house we were inheriting.

For my part I decided to inspect the entire school by visiting every office, classroom, laboratory, dormitory and storeroom before the boys returned from their holiday. I found that there were only two studies available for the senior boys. The captain of the school used one and the only other two prefects used the second. In one of these rooms, I found the punishment book for the previous term. I remember vividly the last three entries:

> 1. For disobeying my order; six strokes of the cane.
> 2. For insolence to me; eight strokes of the cane.
> 3. For using my towel; eight strokes of the cane.

I was dumbfounded. Whilst it was true that as captain of my own school I had been allowed to use the cane, the experience had made me even more determined to make certain that no pupil ever beat another pupil. To my knowledge, this had never happened during my time at Marlborough and I was determined that it would never happen while I was headmaster of any school. I searched the two studies and found a quantity of canes. I removed them and added them to what looked like a horrific store of canes in my own study. I began to wonder what I had unearthed.

I decided to ask the captain of the school, E. J. D. Leadbeater, to return to school early and stay the previous evening in our house so that I could discuss with him his responsibilities, and the way the school was run by the pupils.

I told him that while I was Headmaster of the school no pupil would ever beat another and that he had to understand why that was my philosophy. I felt very sorry for him for, although he was a highly intelligent and charming young man, he had been in the school since he was eight and had grown up in an atmosphere where corporal punishment was taken as the norm. I learnt from him that house prefects used the slipper on other boys, that the prefects had always beaten, that the assistant masters beat, the housemasters beat and, of course, the Headmaster. We spent a long time talking about the problem and I believe he began to understand that there might be an alternative way of disciplining a community. My hopes were, however, slightly shattered when he told me that there would very quickly be a riot if the prefects were not able to beat. I made the only response possible: 'When there is a riot, send for me.'

When the other two prefects returned the next day I felt even more sorry for them as they were thunderstruck by the news. Understandably, their reaction had all the undertones of 'We had this done to us and now it is our turn to do it to them'. Needless to say, they called it a privilege. So began what turned out to be a long process of educating an entire community on different ways of disciplining.

The riot duly arrived on the second day of term. It had been the custom for the whole school to be paraded in the Great Hall and then marched down the central corridor to the dining hall which was situated opposite Chapel. Indeed, for any meal or chapel service this procedure always took place. The whole process had to be completed in silence. That evening, in front of all the pupils, one of the prefects had told one young man to stop talking. The young man concerned did not do so and the prefect, faced with the absence of his cane, was defeated. This was the riot I had to quell.

Accordingly, one of the first things we did was to stop this procedure of marching over 300 pupils around the school in silence. While making the changes I discovered that my predecessor never allowed a boy even to walk down the main corridor as it disturbed him in his study which was situated on the corridor. It was, however, worse than this as the main block of school lavatories was at the opposite end of the school from many of the class-rooms. Therefore, if the boy was to be excused, he either had to walk down the main corridor, which was banned, or walk round the front of the school past the Headmaster's study windows, which was also banned, as it disturbed him once again. The only alternative was to go round the other side of the school, which took far longer. Very quickly, it became apparent to me that we had to change all the school rules. But I could see that I was in great danger of so liberating a community that I would be left with chaos if I did not carry with me my colleagues in the Common Room.

I had not begun all that well with them as I had become incredibly bored at the first Common Room meeting. This took place the day before term began and consisted, according to custom, of the Headmaster and his colleagues going through all the examination results, pupil by pupil, and deciding what their future might be. The results were very poor. My difficulties were increased as I knew none of the pupils by name and each of my colleagues seemed to have an opinion about every child. However, we battled on for a long time through a very large number of names until we got down to the bottom of the alphabet. I remember well one boy called Wilson who had curious results: a pass in English grammar but a fail in English literature; a fail in mathematics but a pass in additional mathematics; a pass in physics but a fail in biology. It seemed to me that here was a boy who was probably intelligent but had done little work and foolishly said 'Does anyone know this silly lad who seems to me to be intelligent but totally lazy'. There was a sudden silence and a long pause until, eventually, the quiet voice of a senior colleague, who was head of biology, and therefore in charge of my own teaching said 'Headmaster, he is my son'. I am glad to say that Edward Wilson and I became good friends, but it was not the way for a young head to start. Indeed, there was only one member of the Common Room who was younger than I was and I found myself volunteering him for every new idea I had!

I knew, of course, that beating was always going to be a great issue for me and it was in about my third week that we reached crisis point. One of the housemasters telephoned to inform me that he was sending a fifteen-year-old pupil to be beaten by. I cannot now remember the reason, but I do remember asking the housemaster why I had to beat the boy. I was informed that the boy had been slippered by the house prefects, caned by the school prefect, caned by assistant masters and caned by the housemaster. None of it had had any effect and it was now my turn. I gently suggested that as none of the other canings had worked perhaps it would be best to do something different. I was informed, very sharply, that this was not possible and that it was my duty to beat the boy, as was the custom in the school. Further, the housemaster told me that he had given the boy eight strokes of the cane and that I would have to match that number so as not to devalue the system. Looking back on the occasion I suppose I should have simply confronted the housemaster and sorted the whole matter out there and then, but he had informed me that he had already told the boy that he was to be beaten by the new Headmaster and that was that. Meekly I requested that the boy be sent to me.

There was a knock on my door and in came as inoffensive-looking a boy as I could imagine. From the moment he set foot in my study I knew there was no question of my touching him. I suppose I must have had a discussion with him about what he had done, but it must have been innocuous as I cannot now recall the offence. I was still playing first-class rugby football and the thought of unleashing a bamboo on this child filled me with horror. However, he knew I was going to beat him and he obediently, and expectantly, touched his toes. I took a cane out of my cupboard and raised the flap of the ginger hacking jacket that all pupils then wore. It so happened that in my study was an old upright padded Parker Knoll chair, although I had no idea how dusty it was until I had beaten it soundly with eight vicious strokes of the cane. Throughout the show the boy touched his toes. Clearly he was counting, for at the end of the eight he stood up and looked at me as if I was totally mad. I said to him, 'You and I now have a problem. I do not know whose is worse. If anyone in this school knows that I have not beaten you then I think your life will not be very easy and I will certainly have to go. However, I have a wife to support and I do not wish to lose my job. Might I suggest, therefore, that you go back into the school and say that it is not a good idea to be sent to the new Headmaster to be beaten and that he is really difficult to cope with'. The young man just looked at me, said nothing and turned to go. As he got to the door I said 'One further thing, could you please just go out there and behave sensibly.' He still said nothing and left my study. I knew I had gambled with my career but I also knew I had faith in young people and, as events turned out, that faith was totally justified. As far as I am aware he never told a soul but I do know that he became a model pupil and that the housemaster was suitably impressed. Of course, the problem was now magnified as I could envisage a whole stream of boys being sent to me to be beaten and I knew I could not carry out the same charade twice! The first item on the agenda for the next housemaster's meeting had been created and the meeting had to be urgent.

After a year at Ellesmere, and during the summer holidays of 1962, our first son, Martin, was born. We had thought long and hard about his name; we did not want it to be shortened easily and with his surname we had to be careful! We had him baptised by the Bishop of Shrewsbury in the Chapel. I had been asked by the Second Master whether any boys could attend and, of course, I said, yes. To Angela's and my amazement and embarrassment the whole Chapel was full. I still think the hard Ellesmere discipline of those days had something to do with it. All went well until the end of term Christmas pantomime when the boys baptised him 'Martini, and hoped he would be dry!' Three other married members of the teaching staff came on to the campus that autumn term—houses having been built for them—raising the total number of resident teacher families from one to four. The tide was turning.

4

The Headmasters' Conference

I SOON realised how grateful I was to my predecessor as he had turned the school into a very efficient business which was making a good surplus and I was therefore in a position to improve facilities and develop the school. He had been appointed Headmaster in 1935 at the request of the senior masters in the school who knew him well as he had been appointed a junior master only a few years earlier. In those days, headmasters had to be ordained and so he left the school for ordination training before returning as its head. He controlled the school during the thirties when recruitment was very difficult. Indeed, there was a time when it looked as if the governors would have to close the school, but he fought against them and worked amazingly hard to save Ellesmere.

For example, he took copies of all the local newspapers and identified the names and addresses of all baby boys who had been born during the week. He then got in his motor car and hand delivered the Ellesmere College prospectus to each home. He controlled the school during the war years but forgot, after the war, to keep up-to-date with educational change and isolated himself in North Shropshire. As a result of this he was unknown to other headmasters and no one had ever met him at meetings, either national or regional, of the Headmasters' Conference. He had also continued the strict post-war saving regime, even when the school was prospering. He still walked around at night with a bag of 40 watt bulbs determined to make certain that nobody wasted electricity. Any bulb with a wattage greater than 40 was removed by him and substituted by one from his bag. Accordingly, although I had to change almost everything within the school, I shall always be grateful that he left me the wherewithal to do it.

I had been informed by the Headmasters' Conference that I was to be elected a member on probation, and the terms of the probation were that the numbers in the sixth form at Ellesmere had to be doubled within two years. At the same time the Governors had given me instructions to move the junior school to separate buildings in Shrewsbury, where they would be looked after by another head, whilst I would be a governor. In this way we could use the junior school buildings at Ellesmere to increase the size of the senior school, but that would not be easy unless there was a constant supply of recruits. An investigation into future registrations showed that, whilst I had a good number for one year, there appeared to be virtually nothing over the following decade. I could see the task was immense. The immediate problem, however, was to replace the twenty-four boys who would be leaving in December. To my delight there were thirty registered to sit the common entrance examination in the November for entry in January, and I realised I had no short-term problems. Or so I thought.

The thirty boys duly sat the common entrance but an analysis of their marks showed that none of them had scored more than 20 per cent average. And this average was correct even after I had ordered all the mathematics marks to be reassessed. The head of mathematics had brought me his common entrance results and I found that no pupil had a positive score against his name. All of them had negative marks and, on discussing this with him, I found that his policy was to subtract a mark for every mistake. Therefore, if a candidate made 115 mistakes he scored minus 15! I had never met any such system before and instructed him to revise the marking process in such a way that we recorded positive numbers, however low. However, even this positive change in policy did not significantly effect the overall average mark of the candidates and I realised that I had a problem on my hands.

I knew that if I accepted twenty-four of these boys into the school I could never ever double the number in the sixth form as the majority were never going to pass enough O-levels to qualify. Indeed, on analysis, I found that most of the boys in the sixth form had all come through our own junior school and that the entry at thirteen nearly always left at O-level as they could not cope with an advanced level syllabus. I decided to fail all thirty candidates.

The effect of this decision was alarming. Preparatory schools from all over the country were telephoning to enquire what had gone wrong. Apparently, no one had ever failed the entry examination to Ellesmere College before. I informed them that the school was under new management and that I was only prepared to accept pupils whom we considered capable of sixth form work. Once the dust had settled I then had to face the prospect of the school having twenty-four fewer pupils than I had promised the Governing Body. The surplus budgeted by my predecessor would more than disappear. My wife and I devised a small form, copies of which were left by all the telephones in our house, my secretary's telephone and my own office telephone. We manned the telephones throughout the rest of November, the whole of December and the beginning of January. I let it be known, through the preparatory school headquarters in London, that I was prepared to accept any child who had scored more than 40 per cent. I knew that there were many who had failed entry to the bigger schools in the south of England whose parents might be looking for a good school for their off-spring. We worked hard. We persuaded a lot of parents from Sussex, Surrey and Hampshire to send their children to Shropshire and I began the January term with a full complement of twenty-four new boys all of whom had scored more than the required 40 per cent.

I continued for several years with this policy of keeping entry into the school through the common entrance examination at above 40%, although we published a 50% pass mark with some pupils being allowed in, in exceptional circumstances, with a lower mark. This was the normal practice in those days and it had meant that the intake into the school improved academically. However, as the years went on, I was fully aware that some of the finest young men in the sixth form had arrived in the school with very low common entrance marks. They had succeeded in overcoming academic problems by people having confidence in them. Even more, they had been encouraged to participate in many activities outside the academic curriculum and, through these activities, had gained in confidence and self-respect, which in turn had a spin-off in improving their attitude to academic work. I fully believed that their IQ had risen during the first three years they were at Ellesmere. It was therefore very important to me that I studied carefully the background of any boy whose marks were low to make absolutely certain I was not missing out on a potential scholar or someone who would otherwise benefit from the type of education that we were offering. Nobody showed this better than young Richard.

Richard's father had been at Ellesmere himself but the boy had a music scholarship to go to Repton from his choir school. However, when he sat common entrance examination he scored less than 20 per cent, with 1% in Latin, and Repton had refused him entry. The father came to   , very embarrassed, asking whether his old school would be prepared to help, despite the fact that he had not made Ellesmere first choice for his son. Naturally, I was prepared to do my best and said that I would like to see all the written reports from his preparatory school as well as the common entrance papers and then I would interview the boy. Having studied the papers I decided to telephone the Headmaster of the choir school. He explained to me that young Richard was a senior choirboy, a soloist and a talented musician, and all of these responsibilities had had a poor effect on his academic work. He had spent so much time singing in the cathedral and carrying out his duties as a chorister that the Headmaster was not surprised by his common entrance marks. I inquired specifically about 1% in the Latin paper, as in those days many candidates succeeded in gaining 100 per cent. I was told by the Headmaster that the master who taught Latin was not very well organised, was often late for, and even missed many classes. Indeed, the Headmaster said he was having difficulties with the man concerned. I sympathised with him and said I would interview Richard.

The boy duly arrived and I was spellbound while he played his cello. He had passed his Associated Board Grade 8 and was clearly very talented. I simply could not see how a young man with such talents could score so poorly in the common entrance exam. I asked him specifically about his 1% in Latin. Richard replied to me that the man who taught him Latin was very often absent and when he was present was often late for a lesson or left before it was over. Satisfied that this confirmed the Headmaster's report I decided that I would certainly give Richard a place in the school. As the boy was leaving my study I asked him who it was who taught him Latin. 'Oh, Sir,' he said 'it is the Headmaster!'

Richard became captain of the school and the only to pupil, while I was Headmaster, to gain an open exhibition in history to Oxford.

My first problem was over, but my second still existed: how to satisfy the Headmasters' Conference that within two years the numbers in the sixth form would double.

We were not helped at that the time by the Advisory Centre for Education in Cambridge, which produced a monthly magazine called *Where*, containing the first league table ever to be published. They had analysed all the previous year's A-level results, turning each of them into a numerical score which they divided into the annual school fee thus producing the *Where* best buy league table. In October 1961 Ellesmere College was next to bottom and this had a devastating effect on the Common Room, the boys and their parents. I was faced with carrying out a lot of work to restore confidence and to attempt damage limitation. The table, of course, only made the Headmasters' Conference more determined to see that we improved our sixth form numbers

Although we had improved the entry at the bottom end of the school at thirteen this was not going to have any effect at all on increasing the sixth form numbers within two years. I decided that there were only two ways to achieve the target and both of those would involve bringing pupils into the sixth form from outside the school. The first way was to recruit foreign students, but I was prepared to do that for a small number only as I did not want to give the school the reputation of being full of foreign students since this would damage the intake at thirteen. The second way was to make the sixth

form co-educational which would double the numbers. Of course, in 1961
there were no girls in the sixth forms of any of the public schools and no one
had ever suggested the idea. It seems obvious now but it was not easy then to
convince the Common Room that this was the way to develop the school.
Faced, however, with the alternatives of expulsion from the Headmaster's
Conference, or girls in the sixth form, the Common Room agreed to support the plan. This was then presented to the Governing Body who required
even more persuasion. Eventually there was total support from both bodies
and I wrote to the Headmaster's Conference to inform them of our plan of
action. By return of the post I received a letter from the Secretary of the
Headmasters' Conference informing me that if Ellesmere College accepted
any girls into the sixth form I would be expelled from the Headmaster's
Conference as it was a conference for boys schools only. It rarely pays to be
ahead of your time, especially in education!

I therefore went back to the drawing board and saw no alternative to a step
which would lead to expulsion from the Headmasters' Conference in 1963.

One of the reasons why the numbers in the sixth form were small was
because the intake at thirteen, with so many scoring below 20 per cent, did
not produce boys capable of progressing beyond O-level into A-level studies.
Indeed, very many of them failed their O-levels first time round and had to
stay on for a further year in order to resit them. These boys had traditionally
been placed in a form called the Upper Fifth while those sitting O-level for
the first time were called the Fifth Form. One evening the solution to my
problem came to me. If I called the Upper Fifth the Lower Sixth, and the
Lower Sixth the Sixth, and the Sixth the Upper Sixth and if I brought in a few
foreign students for good measure, I would double the number in the sixth
form by 1963. The Headmasters' Conference had only asked me to double
the numbers in the sixth form; they had not asked me to double the numbers
sitting A-level examinations. This procedure was carried out, the Headmasters' Conference was satisfied, I remained a member and Ellesmere was
saved. I hasten to say that, with the way the modern Headmasters' Conference is organised, it would be impossible for a young headmaster to get away
with that kind of manipulation of numbers today.

Not that my first meeting with my colleagues of the Midland Division of
the Headmasters' Conference was a great success. I was determined to say
nothing during the actual business meeting. However there was an item on
the agenda concerning the syllabus at 16 for the teaching of French (the old
O-level). There was a movement to increase the amount of oral French and
decrease some of the more complex written grammar; something I was
really enthusiastic about. I heard my colleagues discussing all of this and it

became clear that they were united in opposing any decrease in the written grammar element and, therefore, were opposed to any corresponding increase in the oral element. I heard the chairman saying that he would report back to the HMC Committee that the Division were unanimous in opposing any change. I felt I had to say something. As quietly and quickly as possible, I supported the proposed change emphasising that the ability to communicate orally between peoples was more important than some of the more intricate grammatical conundrums of the French language. There was a silence. The chairman beamed at everyone, and said 'Good, I can therefore report to the main committee that we are unanimous!'

In some ways this has been my relationship with the Headmasters' Conference on many occasions for, despite the fact that I chaired the Conference, I did not always agree with the majority. Maybe this came in part because of my training as a zoologist. I was the first zoologist to become a member of HMC and the first to chair it. In 1961 nearly all my contemporaries in the Conference were classicists or historians and their approach to problems was very different from mine. Today the situation is very different as many heads are scientists.

At my first annual conference at St Andrews I behaved badly. We were being shown round the marine biology laboratories at the university, laboratories I knew by repute but had never before visited, and they were truly magnificent. The department had laid on an excellent exhibition for us all and I was walking around immediately behind three very distinguished headmasters. They were, at that stage, at the top of their profession: Robert Birley, Eton, Desmond Lee, Winchester and Walter Hamilton, Rugby. The former two were knighted sometime after they had finished their headmagisterial careers. As we walked round, studied specimens and looked down microscopes, I overheard their conversation which, to my young ears, was ignorant and infantile. I do not believe that any of them had had a biology lesson at school or, maybe, at any time in their lives. Their conversation seemed to me comparable to that of silly schoolboys. Something within me stirred and, without thinking, I tapped Desmond Lee on the backside as he looked down a microscope and made what was, to me, another inane remark. I said 'Excuse me, but if I were to make remarks about Homer or Ovid along the lines that you are making about my subject I think you would say that I was not fit to be a headmaster.' There was a terrible silence; one looked at me as if I were not there, another turned his scornful eye upon me but said nothing, whilst the third chuckled and smiled at me. No more was said. Many years later, they were all on the Committee of the Governing Bodies Association and I, as a senior headmaster, was addressing them about the future of the sixth form curriculum and public examinations. They appeared to have forgotten my 'insolence' all those years ago, although I had not. They sat, all three of them, in a row at the front and I tried to keep calm as they asked searching questions in the discussion period after my talk, before entertaining me with great warmth. I decided not to remind them of our first meeting at St Andrews.

In 1977 I was asked to give one of the 'key note' addresses to the Conference which was being held at Exeter University. I took the opportunity to attack the proposals from the then Conservative Government for the introduction of Normal and Further Examinations in the sixth form. It was one of the attempts to broaden the curriculum but, in my view, it was misconceived. Incidentally, it was the first time a head had used visual aids when giving a lecture to Conference. The speech attracted a lot of media attention. The *Daily Telegraph* made it their second leader and the *Times Educational Supplement* published all the conclusions very accurately. But, much more importantly, my proposals to be adopted in lieu of the Government's proposed Normal and Further examinations were accepted unanimously by a vote proposed by the then Headmaster of Eton, Michael McCrum. It was the only unanimous vote that I can recall in my thirty years of membership but we have had to wait until this year for some of the proposals to be implemented and one, in particular, I still hope to see introduced. That is a paper at AS level along the same lines as the Theory of Knowledge paper in the International Baccalaureate.

The Conference in 1977 was also remembered within 'the club' for the after dinner speech given by the representative of the host university, who spoke for just over an hour on the history of mathematics, losing his audience at ten o'clock at night after the first fifteen minutes!

In the seventies many of the boys schools started accepting girls into their sixth forms. Some schools acted without any kind of consultation with the girls schools, and understandably, this created quite a lot of ill feeling in the Girls' Schools Association. At that time, when I was Head Master of Lancing prior to that school taking any girls into the sixth form, I was chairman of the Eastern Division of the Headmasters' Conference. I therefore suggested in 1976 that the Division should invite the headmistresses of the girls' schools in our area to a discussion to try and sort out our differences. After all, the problem had been written about in the national press and it was time that we all got together. I did not receive unanimous support from the schools in the Eastern Division which, in those days, stretched from the Channel Islands in the south west to Norfolk in the north east. Nevertheless, we decided to go ahead and arrange a combined meeting.

I wrote to the headmistress who had been most vociferous in her anger that the schools were losing their girls after O-level to the boys' sixth forms. Elizabeth Manners was then Headmistress of Felixstowe Hall in Suffolk and was a very outspoken and determined lady. She was grateful for the invitation and readily agreed to meet us when we were next all gathered in London.

We held our meetings in the East India Club in St James's Square and my colleagues had decided to deal with their normal business first and then welcome the ladies for open joint discussion. I knew the meeting would be very difficult, not only because of the particular issue, but also because some of my members felt that independence meant that they could do exactly as they pleased. They argued that, if the girls schools could not retain their girls in the sixth form, that was their problem and not ours. A great deal of diplomacy would be required.

We had finished our meeting and I was standing by the window of the second floor overlooking St James's Square when I saw the Headmistress of Felixstowe walking into the Square followed by a group of other headmistresses. They all looked remarkably determined and I could not help feeling that the leader was a rather Margaret Rutherford-like figure with the jolly-hockeysticks behind. As soon as that naughty thought entered my head I suddenly realised the appalling mistake that I had made. The East India Club is a men-only club and whilst, today, ladies are met most charmingly at the door, and there is a ladies drawing room upstairs, in those days ladies were refused entry through the doors in St James's Square. I had forgotten to warn the Headmistress of Felixstowe; I had forgotten to warn the hall porter. It was too late for me to do anything.

The hall porter informed the ladies that they could not enter and instructed them to go round the back of the building, enter through the back entrance and then find their way by the back lift to the meeting room on the third floor. I could just imagine the comments made by the headmistresses as they walked round St James's Square and down towards Christie's before turning right to reach the back entrance. I was not mistaken as, by the time they reached our room, steam was almost visibly coming out of their ears. It took rather a long time to settle the meeting and how glad I am that, today, the relationships between the Headmasters' Conference and the Girls' Schools Association are so friendly and creative. Sometimes some things do change for the better.

5

Magistrates and Port

WHILST all this fun and games was going on the within the College and the HMC, I began to be invited to help with the community beyond the school. In particular, I was invited to become a Justice of the Peace in 1963 and, as in those days there was little training, I was able to give some time to the responsibility. There was a very small group of magistrates for the Ellesmere bench in those days: three of the landed gentry; Colonel Kynaston, and Majors Needham and Mowat; Mrs Cholmondeley, the widow of a Major-General; Mrs Thomas, who ran the local choral society, and myself. We served a very rural community where one of the more heinous crimes was allowing your dog to worry the sheep; rarely was there any violence, and burglary was virtually unheard of. Poaching and minor traffic offences were regular items on our monthly bill, whilst the juvenile list was always small as the local Police Sergeant Jarvis kept the youngsters well under control by a mixture of his kindly but fierce voice, and a clip round the ear.

I do recall one famous incident when we had before us a visitor from a different part of England who clearly did not understand our rather feudal approach. For example, we never locked our cars while out shopping. The defendant pleaded not guilty to some crime, and had clearly been very offensive to our Police Sergeant, Sergeant Jarvis. In presenting his case the Sergeant began to explain to the Chairman of the Bench what the defendant had said . . . 'Sir, I do not think that Mrs Cholmondeley should hear what the defendant said; shall I write it down?' 'Certainly Sergeant' said the Chairman and a piece of paper was handed up to the Bench. It was read by those of us who were allowed to do so but dear Mrs. Cholmondeley had the paper turned upside down and slid past her to me so that she could neither hear or read offensive language. We then *all* declared the offender 'guilty'!

I tell the story, because of the difficulty I had with one of my colleague magistrates at the end of my first term as Headmaster. The school was preparing for the carol service, the Christmas concert, the Christmas dinner and the house Christmas parties and I was watching the school being transformed with decorations. One evening I went home with the school looking

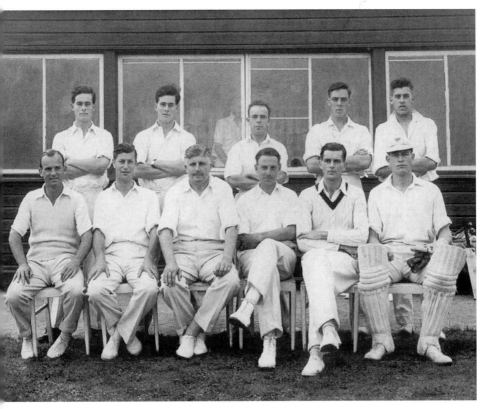

Berlin, July 1950. 1st Battalion. Royal Fusiliers cricket team. The author keeping wicket to the bowling of, amongst others, his Colonel, Cosmo Nevill (Old Harrovian) seated third from left.

Twickenham, 7 December 1954. Leading out the Cambridge XV. Peter Davies, who won the game with his goal kicking follows, with Dennis Silk behind.

Twickenham, 1955. England v. France. The author is standing fifth from the left. W. P. C. Davies, another Headmaster to be, is second from the left.

Marlborough College. Winners of the Public Schools Sevens at Rosslyn Park, April 1957.
J. R. Skinner, P. L. Bell, J. A. Collier, R. H. Stanton, R. E. Matson
I. A. Balding, A. R. Tanner, N. J. Hill-Norton.

40 years later, April 1997.
P. L. Bell, J. A. Collier, R. H. Stanton, J. R. Skinner, the author (coach)
I. A. Balding, A. R. Tanner, Sir Nicholas J. Hill-Norton.

The Tanera Mor party from Marlborough College, April 1960.
J. H. S. Thompson, N. M. Bannerman, B. S. V. Gladstone, J. J. Halliday, the author
P. G. Unwin, J. Critchley, N. D. Maurice.

40 years later, March 2001.
Back row: J. H. S. Thompson (Army officer), B. S. V. Gladstone (TV producer),
J. J. Halliday (Doctor), the author.
Front row: P. G. Unwin (Farmer), J. Critchley (Doctor), N. D. Maurice (Doctor).
(N. M. Bannerman, deceased).

Dr Matanya (Matt) Sampson, the
Ellesmere College School Doctor.

Prize Giving, Ellesmere, June 1963.

The Provost, the Bishop of Shrewsbury,
with Frank Sutterby, housemaster, and
the author listening to the Professor of
Law, Liverpool University.

Ellesmere 1964. Opening of Lambart House, named after the Earl of Cavan's father.
The Earl of Cavan, Mrs Vernon Howard, The Countess of Cavan, Mr Vernon Howard (housemaster),
Sir Offley Wakeman (Chairman of Governors) and Mrs Angela Beer.

Ellesmere, 23 June 1966. The Great Fire. Flames roar through the heavily
timbered ceiling of the dining hall.

Ellesmere, December 1966. The author serving Christmas dinner to members of the non-teaching staff: Tom Edwards, the painter, Eddie Rowe, the cricket professional, and the head gardener.

Ellesmere, 17 May 1969. The re-dedication of the Chapel and opening of the new buildings. The Revd Wilfred Derry, Sir Edward Boyle, the author, The Rt Revd Trevor Huddleston, Lord Bridgeman, Mr Alex Moira (architect) and Sir Offley Wakeman.

Lancing, 10 October 1970. Lieut. General Sir John Evetts OL, Field Marshall Lord Montgomery of Alamein, the author and Mrs Angela Beer.

Professor Stafford Beer, the author's brother, President the World Organisation of Systems and Cybernetics, a the Head Master's House, Lancing.

normal inside and out, but the next morning the interior of the school was transformed with Christmas trees. There must have been at least ten of them, all fine specimens and ready for the boys to have fun decorating.

You will recall that I was Bursar as well as Headmaster and therefore I went to see the accountant to find out under which account the cost of all these Christmas trees was charged. My relationship with the accountant was amazing. Mr Sumsion had fought in the First World War and received an injury which made it difficult for him to stand up, let alone walk. His work was brilliant and he sat in his small office keeping immaculate accounts. The difficulty was that, as I had to sanction all expenditure, and was myself having ideas every other minute which would cost money, I was rushing in and out of his office with monotonous regularity. He was a gentleman of the old school: he liked to be called Sumsion and, whilst I found it difficult, I respected his wish. However, it became very clear to me that he was having difficulty leaping to his feet every time I rushed into his office; it seemed grossly unfair that he should have to put up with this hyperactive young Headmaster, having previously been left alone. Therefore I said to him 'Sumsion, please, there is no need for you to stand every time I enter your study. Please do not do so.' He replied 'Sir, all my life I have had someone to whom I could stand. At the moment, as you are the Headmaster, I would prefer to stand when you enter my office, if you do not mind.' I felt duly chastised.

On this occasion I was met by a blank stare and a few words suggesting complete ignorance of both the existence of any Christmas trees, and certainly the question of any payment for them. I became suspicious and began asking more questions. Housemasters simply told me that it was the tradition at this time every year for Christmas trees to appear. 'No, Headmaster, we have no idea where they come from.' I realised there was only one person who would know the answer and so I sent for the captain of the school. I asked him where the Christmas trees had come from and he sighed; 'Headmaster, you don't really want to know do you?' 'Yes, I do!' And then he told me the extraordinary story.

Yet another of the traditions in this remarkable school was that the boy heads of all the houses went out at about two o'clock in the morning, armed with saws and axes to invade one of the local land owner's plantations. The fact that the owner was Chairman of the local Bench was information that had not, hitherto, been given to the boys. This raiding party then chopped down the finest Christmas trees on his estate and arrived back at the College ready to spring a surprise on the entire community the following morning. The fact that everyone knew where they came from was, apparently, ignored. When I suggested that this was stealing I was ruled out of court.

The captain of the school warned me that if I removed this 'privilege' then it would be the last straw with the senior boys who had felt throughout my first term that their wings were being clipped closer and closer to the bone. I realised that something akin to the judgment of Solomon was required and I retired home to lick my wounds and consider the problem.

I decided that the only thing to do was to face the Chairman of my local Bench and tell him the truth but, as I was the newest recruit to the Bench, I did not feel in a very strong position. I telephoned Colonel Kynaston, made an appointment and called round that evening for a glass of sherry. I had decided to tell him the entire story. He listened to me in amazement and eventually thanked me for solving one of his annual mysteries as he could never understand who had stolen the trees or where they had gone. Naturally, he would never have suspected the College! I apologised to him profusely and asked him whether he would be prepared to accept a case of port for his trees. He thanked me saying that he would not have known anything about it if I had not been to see him and, of course, the matter was now closed. Emboldened, I then took the next step, explaining that this was a tradition which had, apparently, gone on for many years and I was slightly frightened to abolish it in view of all the other changes I had made during that first autumn. Would he be prepared in future years to allow a certain number of his trees to be removed in the early hours of a morning in late December provided that the thieves left a case of port on his front doorstep? He thought for a moment, he chuckled, and then said that he was happy to accept such a proposition on the understanding that the only trees that were chopped down were those that he had previously marked with a white cross. I accepted the suggestion. The following year I explained to the captain of the school and the heads of houses that I was prepared to turn a blind eye to their nocturnal wanderings provided that they took with them my case of port. They were to leave it on the landowner's front doorstep and then chop down only the trees that he had previously marked. The boys were delighted and, as far as I know, the cost of a case of port appears annually in the school accounts today, representing ten or so Christmas trees.

It was a very feudal community and everyone knew everyone else. Those were the days when our telephone number was Ellesmere 7. Whenever I telephoned I had to go through the local exchange and I was usually informed that the person whom I was ringing was dining with Mr and Mrs so-and-so that evening. Therefore I should telephone Ellesmere 'X' if I wanted to speak to them. The people who managed the telephone exchange knew more about the social activities within the neighbourhood than anyone else.

There were many parties and the first we attended I shall never forget. I was the only man present in white tie and tails; all the other men were wearing green silk knee breeches and silver buckles on their shoes. However, everyone was extremely friendly and welcoming whilst we were on a steep learning curve as the old, authoritarian school community could not have been at greater variance with our social world outside of the College.

Toward the end of that first term I realised there might be a social life for the boys as well for we received a splendid invitation to a Christmas Ball at Moreton Hall whose Headmistress at that time was the redoubtable Miss Bronwen Lloyd Williams. She had been a professional dancer in her youth and ran a grand private school for young ladies near Oswestry. She was a complete martinet and ran an establishment which would puzzle present-day Ofsted inspectors. However, very good academic results were achieved and the finest social graces developed. The Director of Education sent his daughter there. On one occasion, concerned about his daughter's academic progress, he wrote to the Headmistress. He received an open postcard, by return, which simply said:

> Received your letter. Don't fuss.
> Yours, Bronwen

When, therefore, Angela and I received the invitation to attend the ball together with thirty of our sixth formers, we readily accepted.

Thirty-one men in their dinner jackets and Angela in her ball gown left the College in the bus with great anticipation. When we arrived all our pupils vanished onto the dance floor whilst Angela and I were taken on one side by Bronwen. To my horror she said 'Ian, come and have a gin with me in my study.' 'But what about Angela?' I said. 'Oh!' she said, 'there are a whole lot of delightful young men here from other schools who would love to dance with her.' Bronwen was clearly someone who was used to being obeyed. The gin in her study turned out to be more a bottle than a glass and, by the time I had reached the dance floor I was well away. Poor Angela had had a more difficult time. She has never looked her age and I suppose the Shrewsbury sixth form should be excused for not realising she was the Headmaster's wife! We wrote our thank-you letters and I received a telephone call from Bronwen asking me whether I had checked all the studies of my sixth formers to make certain they had all received a red rose from one of her girls. Oh dear! If only education were as simple as that . . . I am glad to say that we eventually succeeded, not in abolishing the dances, but in creating, in addition, regular general studies activities in both schools coeducationally every Friday afternoon in the two winter terms.

6

❦❦❦❦❦❦❦❦❦❦❦❦❦❦❦❦❦❦

The Junior School

MY orders on appointment were to plan for the removal of the junior school from Ellesmere to buildings on the outskirts of Shrewsbury. One of the first tasks was to appoint the new headmaster. I was involved with my governors in making the appointment and we got on very well together. However, I had to move some of the existing pupils to Shrewsbury and, of course, all those registered for the junior school in the future. Therefore I had to write to every parent to explain what was happening and why. The majority accepted the decision realising that there would be many benefits to their child from such a plan.

Not all parents, however were totally happy and I did have some very difficult letters to write, as well as interviews in my study which were not always amicable. However, none compared with one exceptional father who was very angry indeed claiming that we had broken a contract. I fully understood his feelings and told him so whilst also explaining why I felt that it was in the best interests of his child in the long run. Never before, or since, have I had to handle such a volcanic reaction from another human being. I can see him now, dressed in a sheepskin coat carrying a riding crop. He lived, I recall, in the centre of Manchester and I very much doubt whether he had seen many sheep or ever handled the riding crop for its proper purpose. On that Saturday morning, however, I learnt that he did have a use for it. After we had discussed the situation reasonably calmly, he began to raise his voice and when he got no further with me began shouting. When this had no effect, he launched himself at me with his riding crop and it was only with a deft move on my part that I escaped decapitation as the crop landed with an enormous thwack across my desk. His wife, a charming lady, asked him to try and calm down a little. He took no notice and launched himself for another attack, which I was able to escape from whilst he shouted 'I played rugby, too, you know. I know how to lose my temper and get my own way!' On hearing that I felt I had a chance and quietly asked, as I dodged another blow, for whom he had played. 'Only the fourth team of my local rugby club', he said, 'nothing as grand as you'. 'If you had controlled yourself you might have been promoted to the second team', I said. He stopped and looked at me. We then had a quieter discussion about rugby football and he seemed to forget his son, but I know he never forgave me for moving the boy.

To make matters worse it turned out that we had appointed the wrong headmaster for the junior school. The governors eventually had to ask him to leave and I do not think he took very kindly to my action in supporting that decision. It so happened that the following summer I was playing golf on a very pleasant course in Pembrokeshire during the summer holidays. I had driven my ball down the fairway, which ran parallel to another fairway coming in the opposite direction. As I was addressing my ball, using a four iron, I was suddenly struck between the shoulder blades with an almighty blow which poleaxed me. A ball from the parallel fairway, which had been struck from fairly close range, had found its mark high on my back. When eventually I regained my senses and struggled to my feet I found myself looking at the headmaster we had just sacked. He very kindly stood me a pint of beer in the bar afterwards but to this day I am not really sure whether he shanked one from the opposite fairway or was a golfer with a hidden talent for extreme accuracy.

Another major problem concerned the salaries of all the masters of the two schools, junior and senior. It transpired that, although there appeared to be an Ellesmere salary scale, it had been almost totally eroded over the years and there was a lot of unhappiness as a result. In the late fifties and the early sixties it was, as now, extremely difficult to recruit science and maths teachers. My predecessor had simply decided to pay all science and maths teachers an extra £150 per year. As my salary as Headmaster was only £1500 it is clear that the extra increment meant a great deal to these teachers; conversely it generated some resentment amongst the rest of the staff. The Common Room was restless. However, it was worse than that, as there was also a group of teachers who, for a variety of reasons, wanted to teach at Ellesmere and had been 'bought in' by my predecessor on the cheap. One or two were being paid well below the correct salary. It was very clear to me that something had to be done fairly urgently.

Obviously I could not reduce anyone's salary and yet the cost of bringing everyone up to their correct rate would have been prohibitive. I had to design a scale, with the judicious use of responsibility allowances, which improved all salaries, but some much more than others. It was not easy and a long period of negotiation took place. Eventually everyone was content and it was possible to augment as my predecessor had left me with sufficient surplus in the annual running of the school. The only organisation that suffered was the school in the Midland Division of the Woodard Schools which had become accustomed to living off the fat of Ellesmere. From 1961 onward, the money which had been generated by prudent management at Ellesmere was used for the benefit of Ellesmere. Today, of course, the Woodard Corporation has changed so that each school is autonomous.

7

Having unsettled the College but not the Chapel

DURING the summer term of my first year I began to realise that I had to be careful not to change the community too much or too fast. I could already see signs of tension and stress, particularly in some of my colleagues who were finding it hard to absorb the changes which were being thrown at them so quickly. I realised that the community could accept a certain amount of change but there would come a point when the stability of a close community might be at risk. Today I wonder how true that may be about many of my colleagues in the maintained schools of the country, as they try to adapt to different governments making endless changes, even before one generation has grown up.

I noticed it in lots of small ways, and it was especially noticeable over discipline. For years young and old alike had been ruled with a rod of iron and now they were being asked to stop, to reflect, to think and to consider how they were behaving. In some ways it is much easier to accept external decisions and grumble about them rather than having to decide for yourself how you are going to behave. Pages of school rules had been scrapped and replaced by just one . . . that you should behave to others as you would expect them to behave towards you. Boys beating boys had been abolished, masters beating boys had been abolished, boys being automatically punished for being low on fortnightly orders had been abolished and I was in discussion with housemasters about the total abolition of the cane. I had not been able never to use it myself as it became clear that, on occasion, the housemasters had to have my support, but they knew I would not continue using it for ever.

Some of the consequences of liberating such a community were bizarre. The captain of the school came to see me one day to complain that I had ruined Chapel. Now this did surprise me for the Chapel was one area that I had simply not touched. The Chaplain had been in the school for a long time and I knew that he was not the right Chaplain for me, nor for new masters that I was beginning to appoint. I could not have a Chaplain in post who had

allowed certain aspects of the previous regime to continue, and I realised
why I had been asked the question about a chaplain at the interview in that
Birmingham hotel. I decided that he had to go. I had seen him privately in
my house and explained to him all the reasons why I felt he should move to
a different post. I emphasised my full support in helping him to move from a
school chaplaincy to a parish or another specialised ministry. We were seated
in armchairs either side of the fire in our drawing room and I can see him
now simply looking at me and saying nothing. For more than fifteen minutes
we looked at each other in total silence. Eventually I said to him that he really
ought to say something in response to my suggestions and his answer was
simply 'It is nothing to do with you. I was appointed by the Provost and only
he can move me.' In a Woodard school the Chaplains are appointed by the
Provost with the agreement of the Headmaster, but in practice the
Headmaster usually presents a chaplain to the Provost who then appoints.
Technically, my Chaplain was correct. Sadly, it took my Provost two more
years to move him and I therefore had a difficult time with a key member of
my staff being in my eyes the wrong person. The difference became somewhat public because, for example, he would preach that it was impossible to
be a practising Christian and believe in the theory of evolution. As I was
teaching A-level biology at the time, and was also preaching in Chapel as a
practising Christian, I need not explain the tension further.

I did not think that the captain of the school was aware of these private dis-
cussions with the Chaplain, but he did know that I had made no changes
whatsoever within the Chapel, with the regularity of services, or the nature
of the services. I asked him why he felt I had 'ruined Chapel', as he put it. He
explained that before my arrival the boys always loved going to chapel as it
was the one place in the school where they could be quiet, escape the atmosphere of the rest of the school and not be punished. Now that I had made the
school a happy place in which to live the boys did not want to go to Chapel
anymore! The picture he painted reminded me of the churches that filled up
during the Second World War in my childhood but emptied again when the
fascist menace had gone away.

The captain of the school and I talked about the issue a great deal. I
realised just how powerful was the influence of the Chapel in the lives of the
boys at the school, founded as it was for the teaching of sound grammar
learning and the Book of Common Prayer. The Chaplain I appointed in my
third year, The Reverend Maurice Gray, remained at Ellesmere until 1998
and, when he retired, the number of pupils who came to pay their respects to
him, and to all that they had received through the Chapel, was movingly
impressive.

However the sermon which has remained most vividly in my mind throughout the last forty–odd years was preached, not in the Ellesmere Chapel, but in Ellesmere parish church. Nor was the sermon preached by the Vicar but by a member of the congregation. In those days, I think it was 1965, the whole College was marched down to the parish church on Remembrance Sunday with the CCF band in front and the boys in uniform. The church was packed with the town and, especially, members of the British Legion. The Vicar preached the sermon; I cannot remember his text but, at one point in his sermon, he said 'if there is an after life' and then emphasised the point by repeating the phrase a second time. At that point an old gentlemen, bedecked with medals, sitting in the rows amongst the members of the British legion, leapt to his feet and shouted out 'Now look 'ere, Vicar, I've not come this morning to listen to you asking whether there is an after life or not. I'm here because I KNOW there is an after life.' And he promptly sat down. There was a silence. The boys were clearly loving it. The Vicar, to his eternal credit, stopped his discourse and said, 'Thank you, Bert, thank you very much. We will now all sing the next hymn.' I hope the boys took the sermon to heart as much as I did.

8

Kurt Hahn

THE money my predecessor had left me was used, in the first place, to create study accommodation for the whole school linked with a new school library. The effect that this had on the academic life of the school, and the improvement in the examination results, was dramatic. This helped to raise the profile of the school and the morale of both the Common Room and the boys so that recruitment from the preparatory schools and from maintained schools became easier. Moreover, I had been able to appoint a large number of new young masters and they transformed Ellesmere into a vibrant, happy and purposeful community. I could not help thinking that my predecessor had probably created a similar establishment shortly after his appointment in the mid-thirties but he had allowed too many masters to stay on too long which eventually resulted in the stagnation I inherited. The men teaching at the top end of the school had been excellent, but were tired. I learnt, after a time, that some were tired because they had tried to change the school and failed, whilst others were tired simply because they were elderly.

I recall in my first term a boy coming to see me asking some simple question which should have been answered by his housemaster. I told him to return to his house and seek the help of his housemaster, but he told me he had already done that and had had the coal scuttle thrown at him. That particular gentleman was aged seventy-five, as in 1961 there was no retirement age. I discussed his future with him and requested that he left the school that year, to which he readily agreed. I later learnt that he left my study and went to the common room to exclaim 'That bloody new Head has just sacked me, and if he hadn't he would be no bloody good for the school at all!' The spirit of the man was still there but he, and others, had to go for the sake of the boys.

In order to stimulate my colleagues I was anxious that they should meet the kind of educationalists that I was privileged to meet when I was away on conferences and courses. Therefore I decided to invite such people into the College to talk to the Common Room so that we could all experience the same kinds of challenges and would be able to discuss ideas presented by someone other than myself. We were fortunate that the school doctor, Matt Samson, was related to Kurt Hahn of Gordonstoun fame. Kurt had not only founded Gordonstoun, but also Salem College in Germany and Atlantic College in Wales. He was one of the few original educational minds before or after the second world war. We managed to get him to accept an invitation to come and address the Common Room. He arrived at about 4 pm and I spent two hours talking with him as we walked around the school and its grounds. I suppose that at that time I needed someone on whom to pour out all the tensions and stresses that had built up during my first terms and I fear that Kurt took the strain. After I had been talking for a very long time he eventually turned to me and said 'Now tell me, who is it who disagrees with you? The masters or the governors?' It was a very good question as the governors had left me very free to do as I wished. Looking back, I think I'd probably ridden roughshod too often over both them and the masters.

With that one question he taught me as much as the boy during my earlier career who woke me at three in the morning to explain that he wished to speak with me. I struggled out of bed, put on my dressing down and went into my study to listen again to this young man, aged fourteen, who had been causing me a lot of trouble in my House. I asked him what was the matter and he said 'The trouble with you is that you want me to be like you, and I want me to be like myself.' I believe that I became a better school-teacher after that particular confrontation.

My wife had arranged and cooked, as usual, a dinner to entertain Kurt Hahn and was slightly taken aback when he said to her 'Angela, before I give any talk I like to lie in the dark on my bed for two hours! After the talk, then I like to eat my muesli!' So we had a good dinner party in the absence of our chief guest whilst one topic of conversation was to speculate on what muesli might be. Remember, this was 1963.

I have a tape of the talk he gave that evening expressing his views on how to educate adolescent children. I believe it to be the only tape of this kind in existence and, of course, he explained the philosophy behind the system of education which he had created at Gordonstoun as well as Salem in Germany. Possibly partly as a result of the talk, but also no doubt greatly stimulated by the surrounding countryside and my encouragement, the masters began to organise many more outdoor expeditions and started outward-bound training, especially canoeing. These outward-looking activities broke down something of the inwardness of the previous regime and provided challenges for both boys and adults.

I recall being interrupted in the middle of a Saturday evening school concert by an urgent message concerning an incident in Snowdonia whilst boys were out on adventure training for the weekend. Despite all the training the boys had been given, there had been a serious accident. Three boys were camping on the side of a mountain in very poor weather when they had changed the gas cylinder on their gas heater while they were in the tent. The heater had exploded, destroying the tent, melting their radio, damaging all their equipment and leaving themselves to be transported by emergency transport to the burns unit in South Wales. My journey there was horrific, not knowing what to expect. They, and we, were fortunate in that they all recovered. Their parents were amazingly supportive, not only of their sons, but of the school. I can only be thankful that I taught when I did, as the modern parent is not nearly so understanding about the risks it may be necessary to take if a child is to be properly challenged during adolescence. Kurt Hahn's philosophy, as expounded by him to my colleagues in 1963, would nowadays be heavily criticised, for he believed that each young person should be pushed to almost breaking point in order to find him or herself. I find myself more in sympathy with Hahn than with our overprotective society today.

Another parent, the father of Nicholas Jones (known as Jones 'half dozen' for there were about nine Joneses in the College) was a priest in the Church of Wales, and he had understood my desire to expose pupils to as much outward bound activity as possible. He had been appointed the Vicar of Penmachno, a small village on the edge of Snowdonia. At the top of the valley, Cwm Penmachno, he had a daughter church, which had previously served the miners in the slate quarries in that area. It was now redundant. He had talked with the Church of Wales and came to see me one Saturday morning. To my amazement he offered the College the church for £150. I had neither the money nor the authority to accept, but readily did so. With one or two colleagues we drove to Cwm Penmachno and were delighted by what we saw. Today the old church is an outward bound centre used by the College and hired out to other schools and climbers when the College does not use it.

We were equally lucky during a long spate of infectious absenteeism which suddenly struck the school. For reasons which I have never understood it suddenly became fashionable with the young to run away when they had a problem. Suddenly I found a boy missing for twelve hours, or twenty–four hours, or even longer.

One boy I remember particularly clearly. He had been behaving very badly at his preparatory school and had, on one occasion, run away creating havoc and panic in the school. They found him many hours later hiding in the bush by the side of the front door of the school. He had clearly enjoyed watching the panic he had created. When he arrived with me he still had huge emotional and personal problems and he ran away fairly early in his career at Ellesmere. He was away for more than twenty-four hours and, on his return, was in no fit state to go into the school. My wife, not for the first or last time in our headmastering career together, took the boy under her wing and rested and fed him in one of our spare rooms. He apologised to her for not bringing his dirty crockery downstairs as the blisters on his feet would not allow him to walk. We all knew we had a major problem with this young man.

I was fortunate to have Dr Matt Samson as the school doctor. He was way ahead of his time and freely discussed with me the possibility of the boy seeing a child psychiatrist, something few school doctors would have done. The parents approved, and the boy was seen by another wonderful doctor, Dr David Enoch. The boy immediately became friends with both the doctors and, although he had regular appointments with Dr Enoch, he used to come round to my house every now and again to say he wished to see his psychiatrist . . . now! I always let him go and I recall an evening when he came back from such a visit and said to me 'I think, Sir, I am a lot better. It is now time for my father to see the psychiatrist!' I knew then that all might be well. And so it proved. Twenty years later I received a letter from the boy, telling me of his successful career as a solicitor. He was convinced that if we had not allowed him to see a psychiatrist in those early days, he would have committed suicide. Dr Matt Samson is, alas, now dead; I keep in touch with Dr David Enoch who lives in South Wales and I would love another letter from the young man whose address I have now lost.

The stress and strain on everyone at this time was horrendous, especially so because the school was surrounded by the beautiful meres of North Shropshire, meres which became dangerous, moody deep pools tempting your imagination to run wild whenever a child was missing. Maybe it was something to do with the spirit of the age, the 'swinging sixties', or maybe I had caused too many of the boys to think for themselves during this period of liberating the community. I decided the only thing to do was to tackle the problem head on and one Friday morning I addressed the whole school about the problem of measles and how infectious it was. I then compared the measles to running away when you have a problem and requested that between us all we stopped the infection. To my amazement the problem disappeared as suddenly and as quickly as it had appeared.

But in those difficult days toward the end of the sixties it was not only the young who had their problems and behaved curiously. One boy, whose parents I knew had matrimonial problems, was behaving very badly. It was affecting not only his work but the work and behaviour of others. I therefore asked to see the parents one Saturday morning. On the Friday evening the mother telephoned me to explain that she and her husband were having difficulties and that they had decided on a divorce. I expressed my sadness but at the same time said that I thought it might help their boy as at least he might now try to understand the situation rather than face rows at home which he did not understand. She agreed and said she looked forward to the following morning.

When I met them we had a long talk about the boy but no mention was made of a divorce. Foolishly, as it turned out, I said that I thought the boy might be helped once the divorce had gone through. The father exclaimed 'What divorce?!' I then realised that the mother had used me to tell her husband that she wished for a divorce. That day I missed my lunch and became a temporary unpaid marriage guidance counsellor.

The upshot was that the divorce went through and we agreed that their son would be best off in a day school living with mother. I arranged the transfer to a very good day school where I knew the headmaster, and the parents were pleased. I heard no more until the end of the following term when my friend the headmaster telephoned me to tell me how the boy had progressed. He thought that I should know that the previous evening the boy had broken into the school and burnt down his study. I worry to this day about my inadequate part in this sorry saga, and, indeed, what happened to the poor child.

On another occasion, I had been less worried about a certain fifteen-year-old but he was, nevertheless, on my mind as I walked out of my study to go to lunch one Saturday. I immediately bumped into his parents. They were mightily impressed that I knew who they were, and I felt rather pleased with myself. I started talking with them and found they were equally concerned. I took them for a long walk around the grounds and when we eventually said farewell they were too generous to me. 'It was so wonderful that you knew who we were, and knew so much about John. We have so much confidence that all will now be well. Thank you.' I walked away and then had a sudden panic. I went to my study where I had photographs of individual pupils and I looked John up in the record. I had been talking about the wrong boy! I had mistaken the identity of the parents. But the boys of both sets of parents were the same age, and I could have been equally worried about both. I reflected that all fifteen-year-olds face similar problems and decided that my analysis to the parents of their son may not have been too inaccurate. I let the situation rest. Eventually the two boys came to their senses and became charming young men. Never again have I talked to parents about their son or daughter without first checking the parents' identity carefully.

On a slightly lighter note I recall once being awoken in bed by the police asking me whether I had a sixth form pupil of a certain name and why he did not have a rear light on his bicycle. I had to confess that I had no idea but that I was more interested in knowing what he was doing on his bicycle at three o'clock in the morning. It transpired that he was returning from his engagement party to the barmaid at the local pub. When I approached the parents about this extraordinary story I found that they had been at the party, and a very good party it was, they said!

9

❧❧❧❧❧❧❧❧❧❧❧❧❧❧❧❧❧❧❧❧

Fires

THE first of our three fires took place during our first year, before our children were born, in the early hours of one morning. We were asleep at home when I awoke thinking that a burglary was taking place. There was a rustling and crackling noise downstairs. I leapt out of bed, put on my dressing gown and went out on to the landing to go down the stairs. I immediately realised that there was a serious fire as the centre of the house was full of smoke. It appeared to be coming from the kitchen, and when I opened the door found that the cupboard above the main stove was fully alight and the flames spreading. I shut the door and immediately telephoned for the fire brigade before returning to the kitchen and attaching a hosepipe to the back kitchen tap. I used this to put out the fire whilst creating an enormous amount of black smoke. At about the same time the fire brigade arrived and took charge. They tramped backwards and forwards spreading soot and water everywhere until they eventually told me that all was well.

I was, however, given a sound ticking off by the fire chief, who informed me that the fire had been caused by an electrical fault and that I could have electrocuted myself by spraying it with water. I was told never to do it again!

The following morning one of the senior housemasters asked me how the party in my house had gone the previous day. I told him that there had been no party, but it became clear that many masters had assumed that the noise of the fire, the presence of the fire brigade and shouting all meant that the Headmaster and his wife had had yet another of their joyous parties until the early hours of the morning! None of them would believe my story until they came to witness the damage themselves.

The second fire at Ellesmere was more serious. It occurred on 23 June 1966. I had been invited to go to London to be interviewed in the Jerusalem Chamber of Westminster Abbey as a possible Headmaster for Rugby School the following year. My wife was with me and we travelled back in the early evening from London to Shrewsbury station. We then drove from Shrewsbury to Ellesmere. As we left Ellesmere town itself we noticed a huge pall of black smoke in the sky and I turned to Angela and said it looked as if

Mr Edwards's hayrick had caught fire. However, as we drove closer to the College we both began to have our doubts. As soon as we saw Sergeant Jarvis of the local police standing at the end of the College drive waiting to intercept us, we knew there was a problem. By his side was a great friend of Angela's. She immediately said that no one was hurt, our two children and everyone else was safe. Sergeant Jarvis, however, simply said that I had lost a large amount of the College. We drove on and the sight before us was a remarkable one. The whole of the right side of the College had no roof and smoke was still pouring out from the shell of the big red brick buildings. What had once been a chapel, a magnificent hammer beamed dining hall, house playrooms, domestic quarters and kitchens were now no more than a smouldering mess. Many fire engines were parked around the buildings with snakes of hosepipes meandering around the quadrangle. Water was everywhere. And standing in the middle of this mess was the Bishop of Shrewsbury, William Parker, Ellesmere's Provost. He looked miserable, tired and drained. Indeed, everyone I met looked emotionally and physically exhausted. At that moment I felt grateful to the governors of Rugby School, as I could have done nothing had I been present at the time of the fire, but now the community clearly needed someone to take charge and make decisions.

It turned out that the fire had started in the roof space between the Chapel and the Dining Hall; the area had just been re-wired and the fire was started by an electrical fault. And I had assumed, from the moment I saw the fire, that it must have been boys smoking. I should have had more faith in boys but less in electricians.

I told the Bishop that he might as well go home; he had done his bit and now it was my turn. Fortunately, he agreed and I waved him goodbye as I stood there and racked my brains wondering what to do next. The moment I heard from housemasters, and some pupils, that the boys best be sent home I knew at once that I had to take action to prevent any such decision. I therefore requested that everyone should get on with their evening's study and I would send round details of plans as soon as I had made them. We had to make emergency plans at once for two dormitories of boys who had to be evacuated for fear the building would collapse, and we had to feed the whole community the next day.

At home I suddenly became very grateful, not for the first time, for my experience during National Service. The army had taught me a great deal and now I had an opportunity to put some of that experience into practice. By sheer chance I was fortunate enough two weeks previously to have dined with the General commanding the western region of the army, Major

General Peter Gillett. I telephoned him at 10.30 p.m. and, apologising for troubling him, explained that I had had a major fire at the College. He was intrigued to hear details as he had heard from someone else that some cinema screens in the North Midlands had been interrupted with a newsflash giving details of the fire. I knew then that I was going to have difficulty with the media and so it proved. However, my first concern was to get help and I asked the General whether he could give it to me. He was truly magnificent. He said 'You have my permission to telephone anyone under my command and inform them that your orders are my orders. You will find the appropriate telephone numbers in the telephone book. I am now going to bed but I think you have some work to do. Get on with it!' I was to meet him again on several occasions as he became, on retirement, the senior Military Knight at Windsor, by then Lieutenant General Sir Peter Gillett.

I have to confess that I enjoyed the next few hours. I had been instructed for my Commission in the army from January to April 1950 at Eaton Hall Officer Cadet School, the home of the Duke of Westminster, who was later to become one of my Governors at Harrow School. I had become Senior Under Officer there and received the Sword of Honour, but not before I was nearly cashiered. The cadets had become lazy and were attending breakfast in casual clothes, indeed some in dressing gowns, when the Commandant came to inspect. I was immediately informed that for the next ten days everyone would parade in full battle dress before breakfast and be inspected by me. This was not a popular move. On the penultimate day, the Junior Under Officer in charge of the guards platoon came to see me to request that, as they had to see the tailor immediately after breakfast, could they parade without their boots and gaiters? It was a simple request and, as I knew they had to wear shoes for the tailor, I agreed to it. However, the Commandant decided to come and inspect that morning and he went ballistic. 'Who gave this order?' 'I did', I replied. 'Arrest that man!' was the order. I was locked up for part of the morning and brought before the Commandant who did not take kindly to my having gone against his orders. He declared that the whole Officer Cadet School would continue to parade in full dress before breakfast for another week. 'Dismiss!' I was dumbfounded and immediately said that it was my responsibility, not that of my colleagues, and that his punishment was unfair. If he wanted to punish, he must punish me. He looked at me sharply and said 'Then that is the end of your Commission.' I gulped and repeated that I was the one responsible, no one else. Suddenly, he banged on the table. 'Good,' he said, 'dismiss!' And that was the last I ever heard of it, duly receiving my silver cup at the end of the course. It was a good lesson to have learnt and I remembered it, on occasion, when punishing prefects. It all came back to me that evening as I gave the orders on behalf of the General.

I telephoned the Royal Army Ordinance Corps, the Royal Army Service Corps and the Royal Corps of Signals and summoned officers to my house for an 'O' group at two in the morning of the 24 June. I think the serving officers were quite glad to have a crisis and the means to help. I told them that I wanted breakfast for over 400 people at 0715 hours that morning and then three meals a day, until further notice. I told them that all the crockery and cutlery were destroyed. The college had used metal plates and metal drinking mugs. My predecessor, quite rightly, had reckoned that the boys could never destroy them so nothing had to be replaced. I had tried to persuade my governing body to sell them and allow me to buy china crockery but my request was refused. You can imagine my delight on peering down the lift shaft in the dining hall to see a solid block of steel. All the plates and mugs had melted. This was the first 'present' that the fire was going to give me.

I sent instructions round to the housemasters stating that breakfast would be served on the golf course between 7.15 a.m. and 8.00 a.m., followed by prayers in the Great Hall at 8.30 a.m. and lessons as usual. I then went to bed.

I was up early and on the golf course before any of the boys or masters. Fortunately, it was a beautiful sunny morning and the army had done brilliantly with their field kitchens. Needless to say the press were there and the boys did not let them down. 'This is the best breakfast I have had since I arrived at Ellesmere College' was typical of the kind of remark which was published in the papers the next day. The local and national press were, in fact, very sympathetic and very accurate, with one exception.

A reporter from one of the national newspapers who had caused me a lot of problems in the early hours of the morning, and to whom I had been very polite, had used the occasion to try to make his name. He used the information I gave him to create headlines on the front page of his national newspaper suggesting that Ellesmere College would have to close. I spent the first hour of the following day on the telephone trying to get to the Editor. Eventually I traced him and made my complaint. He promised to make an immediate inquiry. He then telephoned me back to inform me that if I got copy to him within the next hour then that copy, provided it was no longer than the article printed by the newspaper that morning, would be printed on the front page the next day. I thanked him profusely. I used the opportunity to tell the story of an experience that very morning with parents who were considering sending their boys to Ellesmere, and to add that all our silver cups for sporting competitions had been destroyed in the fire, so that I would welcome any gifts from the general public. I received them.

The story I told was of Mr Smith who had a prior engagement to see me about sending his three sons from a Grammar School in Yorkshire to Ellesmere the following year. I was greatly concerned about the visit but it was too late to cancel. I talked with him and I wandered around the school with him picking through the debris. With him I found the only remnant of the organ in the chapel, a few pieces of molten metal. I had the pieces mounted on a wooden base and still have them today as a reminder of the great fire. There was little doubt in my mind that I had lost three very good potential scholars but somehow I maintained my enthusiasm for the future. When he told me that he thought the school would go from strength to strength and that he had no hesitation whatsoever in signing up his three boys there and then, I could hardly believe my ears. I rejoiced and felt that the future really did beckon and I am forever in his debt. I had a story to encourage my colleagues and our spirits lifted. The three boys did come to Ellesmere and all did very well indeed.

They did as well, in fact, as the American boy whose father was looking for a school for him at that time. He had heard of Ellesmere and arrived by helicopter on the lawns outside my study. He talked with me for thirty minutes, told me he wanted his thirteen-year-old boy to come to the school and said he had to go. I said, would he not like to see the school (or what was left of it) and he said yes. The next boy on the rota for showing parents around was summoned and as I closed my door behind the two of them I heard the father say 'Now, I've got just three minutes!' The roar of the helicopter blades disturbed our peace five minutes later. The boy duly arrived and was a huge success.

I spoke to the school the morning after the fire when morning chapel was over and told the boys and staff that there should be no disruption of school routine at all. They would be having their meals at normal times on the golf course, until we had arranged for tables and chairs to be placed in the gymnasium where they would then be eating on a shift basis house by house. The army was magnificent and by its actions probably influenced several pupils to join at a later date. Amazingly, I had a letter from the army years later which was forwarded to me at my next school, Lancing, requesting that I sign the necessary forms as I had requested assistance. I was terrified that the cost would bankrupt the school but, on turning to the forms found that they were yellowing and brown at the edges. They were all headed 'War Emergency Forms'. I signed them all, returned them to the issuing authority and heard no more.

Apart from the press, who were a nuisance, I was bombarded by another type of person whom I had never met before. I was taken totally unawares when all the organ building firms in the country were on the telephone to me the morning after the fire to inquire whether they could quote for the rebuilding of the organ in the chapel. I gathered from them that the number of new organs being built in the UK was so small that they were all desperate for orders.

The loss adjusters for the insurance company arrived very quickly and I spent a great deal of time with them as we attempted to settle the most complex of insurance claims. Fortunately, by this time the College had a Bursar as the wonderful Sumsion, the accountant, had retired a few years earlier. Much of this work was therefore taken off my shoulders. Two things in particular remain in my memory. The first were the claims that the boys could make for loss of their property in the fire. The loss adjustors simply asked any boy who had lost anything to present the Headmaster with a note of the full details. The number of full sets of golf clubs consumed by the fire was truly remarkable. We learnt a lot about the boys. I was with the Chaplain, Maurice Gray, in my house when one of the boys arrived with a list which both of us knew to be pretty bogus. Having been firmly ticked off by me and the Chaplain, and having had his paper torn up, the boy turned to the Chaplain said 'And you, Sir, have presumably presented the Headmaster with a request for a new chapel?' Indeed he had, and it was what he eventually received.

I was concerned about the portraits of all my predecessors, and of some of the governors, all of which had been burnt. How would we replace them? Fortunately the history of the College had been written and there were photographs of the men concerned, or photographs of their portraits. I had these copied and discussed the problem with an art college in Liverpool. They asked some students to paint the portraits in the manner that they might have been painted in the 19th and 20th centuries. These portraits, which cost so little, are hanging to this day. One is brilliant, most are good efforts and one is definitely not to my taste. But at least they are complete.

Morale in the school was higher than at any point before or after. There is no doubt that adversity brought the best out of every man and woman at Ellesmere of whatever age. The parents, too, were brilliant. One in particular was especially important as he made it possible at the end of the summer term to bridge the gap between the departure of the army and the creation of the new temporary kitchen for the beginning of the September term. He erected tarpaulins over what was left of the old burned-out kitchen so enabling us to feed the pupils in the gymnasium during the last week of July. In the terms to follow we had many frustrating problems to solve with temporary feeding arrangements and dining halls.

I used to take my breakfast with the boys in the gymnasium every morning. In September and October it was not so bad, but as we entered November and December I found that struggling from my house in the dark, often in the rain, across to the gymnasium for a not very good breakfast at 7.15 a.m. was getting me down. So how did I react when, one morning, returning from breakfast a young man caught me up and said 'Sir, do you come to breakfast every morning just to show us that if you can put up with it we can put up with it?' I muttered something like 'Well, er . . . I suppose so.' 'That is daft' he replied 'you are the only person in the school who can have a decent breakfast, so you jolly well ought to.' He shattered my resolve.

The outcome for the College was extremely beneficial. We had been well insured. The building which had been the dining hall was so vast that it was possible to place a gymnasium in the basement of the new dining hall and above it two floors of private studies so that my desire to give the pupils more private study areas became a reality.

On 17 May 1969, nearly three years after the fire, The Right Reverend Trevor Huddlestone preached at a celebratory Sung Eucharist and Sir Edward Boyle opened the secular buildings.

Following the great fire we had organised a fire fighting brigade just in case we should ever have another problem. Little did I realise how quickly that brigade would be called into action. I was summoned one evening by the head of science to the main chemistry laboratory which was situated on the first floor in one of the main wings of the school with dormitory accommodation above it for sixty pupils. The small emergency fire brigade was outside the door and the head of science was waiting for me whilst peering through a small glass panel into the laboratory. The end of the laboratory was ablaze and the room was filled with smoke. The boys outside had the necessary equipment whilst I was told by the Head of Science that I had to be very careful. On inquiring what was the matter he informed me that inside the laboratory was a mobile rack of cylinders of oxygen and hydrogen but he could not remember where they were! We both realised that if the fire were not put out immediately the cylinders were likely to explode and if they did I felt certain that the end of the building would be totally destroyed including the floor above. We dismissed the boys, wrapped wet towels around our faces, crawled into the laboratory and sprayed water at the fire. Rows of reagents had been placed on the shelves above the benches; they went down like bottles at a fun fair. After about five minutes the fire had been extinguished and we immediately searched for the rack of gases. Fortunately, they were some distance from the fire and all was well, but I was not pleased by the fire brigade's report on the event. A charcoal block used for oxidising mercury had caused the fire. The charcoal block had continued to stay warm and had ignited itself in the cupboard in which it had been placed.

I began to wonder what kind of pestilence had hit North Shropshire and I was concerned lest I became too well known as a fire-raiser. Amazingly, my concern was answered two months later when a freak storm hit Ellesmere and the entire quadrangle of the school was flooded. The water flooded the basement of the buildings and all the rooms on the ground floor of the main corridor including my own study. The boys were canoeing on a huge lake until the fire brigade succeeded in pumping the water away. This time the fire chief could not make any criticisms of me.

10

The Stress of Teaching

CARING for a complex school community does not mean just caring for the pupils. My colleagues also required a great deal of love and attention, encouragement and challenge. I have already explained that I was able to appoint quite a number of young teachers, having inherited an elderly Common Room. These young teachers did not receive the kind of professional help and guidance which is now not only available but compulsory for new teachers in schools today. Their head of department and other colleagues cared for them, but in a rather haphazard manner and certainly not involving the completion of any forms. Looking back I often wonder whether I really supported them enough, although many of them went on to take positions of greater responsibility and, indeed, headships. One young man, in particular, stands out as he worked so hard to do well in his first year and was an excellent teacher. Sadly, when he was out shopping he took leave of his senses and, despite the fact that he had a lot of money in his pocket, he walked out of WH Smith with an ordinance survey map in his hand for which he had not paid. He was apprehended and handed over to the police who charged him for shoplifting. As a magistrate I knew the scenario pretty well, as we had had other perfectly honest citizens before us for shoplifting unable to explain their actions.

He immediately came to see me and I could sense what I probably should have seen before, namely, that he was extremely tired and under great stress. He had just got married, he had just started teaching, he was contributing an extraordinary number of hours to his pupils and something had to give.

The manager of the WH Smith Oswestry branch informed me that he had no authority to do anything but report the matter to the police. It was not in his remit to withdraw the charge. I went to see the chief executive in London and pleaded with him to withdraw the charge on the grounds that if the situation were to become public he would lose his teaching job and the profession could not afford to lose a man of such quality. I was told this would be impossible and that the law must take its course.

I was determined to stand by the young man and he was equally determined not to bring the school into disrepute. Therefore he agreed that his resignation would be in my hand were the story to become known. At that time, the only people who knew were myself, the young master, his wife, the shop and the police. Fortunately, it was the end of the summer term and it was clear that the case would come before the Oswestry magistrates in the holiday. Together we created a plan.

Once the date of the case was known he would take his wife out of the country on holiday for two weeks. Whilst on holiday he would write post-cards to all his friends in the College and friends in the neighbourhood so that his wife could post them from abroad at the time of the trial. He would fly back to England and I would collect him from the airport and drive him to the magistrates court in Oswestry. He had given his correct name, of course, but because he owned a house away from Ellesmere had given that address for all correspondence. He therefore appeared in court without an Ellesmere address but with his proper name.

I collected him from the airport and drove to the court. He pleaded guilty, was fined and I drove him back to the airport. We then waited to see what would happen next. A brief report in the local paper was picked up by one master, who commented how extraordinary it was that someone of the same surname as one of his colleagues had been convicted of shoplifting. 'Could not have been our man, however, because he was on holiday abroad.'

The young man returned the next term, continued learning his trade as a fine teacher and was appointed to another school, his career saved.

I was much more fortunate with another young man who impressed me greatly at interview but caused problems after I had appointed him. Everyone had returned to the College for the start of the new school year the previous evening. The senior master telephoned me at 7.30 a.m. the following morning to say that someone had already run away. I immediately asked the senior master to get in his car, drive to the boy's home, talk with the mother and bring the boy back to school. But my senior master said 'Oh no, Headmaster, it is not a boy but one of the new masters!' He had left me a note. This said that, as he, the master, was not sure about the true nature of historical truth he did not believe that he should be teaching history to young people. I told the senior master that my original instruction still stood. So the senior master drove to the young master's home, saw his mother and the master was brought back to the College. The young master concerned is now a very fine teacher in another school.

In 1964 we took some of the stress out of teaching boys who had failed O-level mathematics more than once by introducing a primitive computer. This was a simple but effective machine. We had the software for the O-level mathematics syllabus installed and the machine was placed in a small vestibule which was always available to the boys as the public telephone was in the same place. A boy would simply play through the programme, which speeded up, or slowed down, according to his reaction time. If he gave the wrong answer he was taken back a few steps and had the error of his ways pointed out to him. It saved a lot of teaching time and helped many to pass their maths O-level, at that time a requirement for almost any higher education or career prospect.

11

The School Council, 'Any Questions?' and Drugs

IN 1965 the Headmaster's Conference, in order to keep me busy and, perhaps, to keep me quiet, nominated me as one of their two representatives on the Schools Council. This was a quango which had been set up by the then Labour government to control O- and A-level examinations, and advise the government generally on educational matters. I found most of the work extremely boring but one incident taught me a great deal. About forty of us had assembled for a committee meeting, when the chairman announced that we needed three more elected members. He then made three entirely valid points:

1. The representation of women on the Council was minimal.
2. The representation from Wales was minimal.
3. The representation from primary assistant teachers was out of balance with head-teachers.

He therefore suggested that we should consider three ladies from Wales who were primary school teachers. The logic was irrefutable and a representative from the National Union of Teachers leapt to his feet and proposed three candidates who fitted the bill exactly. They were all elected and the National Union of Teachers then had a majority vote in the committee. I was the one independent voice on that committee; the Headmaster of Eton was in a similar position on another committee. He made his name by being reported in the national press as describing some new government plan as 'a dog's breakfast.' I have seldom rejoiced so much as on the day when a later government abolished all the committees of the Schools Council.

I was also at this time increasingly being invited to speak at dinners. On one occasion I was due to speak in Manchester but left Ellesmere too late and arrived at the dinner when everyone was well into their second course. I had therefore not been properly introduced to the people on the top table. I was the fourth speaker replying for the guests. Four days previously I had been at a dinner in London where I heard three new and extremely funny jokes from a member of the Cabinet. I had decided to use these three stories in my thank-you speech. The second speaker told one of the stories and the third speaker told the second and then the third immediately before he sat down. I turned to the chap on my right and said 'I have always wanted to sit next to the chap who has just had his three funny stories told before him and now you have the privilege!' I somehow got through my speech and returned to Shropshire.

The following week there was an urgent telephone call from the BBC and I found myself talking to the producer of 'Any Questions?' who invited me to join the panel, at the last moment, at Ross on Wye for a live radio broadcast. I was astonished and flattered and accepted. The panel dined with Freddie Grisewood, who was question master in those days, in a hotel in Ross. I was introduced to Baroness Stock, Lord Soper and a Mr Joyce who was a well-known prison governor on the Isle of Wight. Eventually we went into the village hall and went on air. I recall very well bowing my head, and desperately hoping that Freddie would not ask me the first question. He didn't, but when it came to my turn I found that the others had said precisely what I had, after racking my brains, decided I would say. It therefore came as no surprise when on asking Freddie afterwards why I had been invited, I was told that at the dinner in Manchester I had been sitting next to the head of the BBC light entertainment programmes! I continued on the panel for several months, including the week David Frost made his first appearance, but it did not help my mailbag as everyone seemed to think that as a headmaster I should have said something different from what I actually did say. However, I did enjoy listening to the repeat on Sundays whilst I was cutting the roast at lunch, knowing that I was being paid for it.

The sixties decade was not an easy time for many institutions. We had witnessed the arrival of the Beatles with what was then considered to be their outrageously long hair. There were the student riots in Paris, the drug and 'love-in' revolution that took place at Woodstock in America, whilst our own young were spreading their wings and challenging authority. Their rebellion was apparent in many ways. The Headmaster of Westminster, John Carleton, concerned that his pupils were staying out too late on Saturday and Sunday evenings, wrote to all parents asking that the boys should go to bed reasonably early on Sunday nights. On the first Monday morning after this request all the pupils sat down outside the school and refused to go to classes because the headmaster was interfering with their private lives. At Oundle, where I went to preach, the authorities found that the cross on the altar had been removed during the Saturday night. Some young people were purposely injuring themselves, others were experimenting in all kinds of wild ways. Authority was under threat and senior boys often decided that it was not their job to tell a younger boy how to behave. The increase in smoking and drinking became a regular topic of conversation among headmasters. The problem of drugs, had, thank goodness, not yet arrived...so we believed.

I was therefore very shocked when in 1968 a sixth form pupil came to see me late one afternoon to inform me that a slightly younger boy in the school had cannabis in his possession and had used it. Understandably, my informant asked for total confidentiality but was equally anxious that I should take immediate action.

Not for the first time, when in a crisis, I asked Dr Matt Samson to come and see me. We sat in my study and wondered what we should do. I decided that although neither of us had any experience of cannabis it was essential that we took action at once. I therefore sent a discreet message through a trusted senior boy requesting that the alleged drug-taker report to my study immediately. He was having supper in the dining hall.

A knock on my door and in he came. I immediately challenged him with the possession of cannabis. He stoutly denied it. I had been warned by my informant that he would probably deny that he had the cannabis as he felt safe with the package sewn into the lining of his jacket. Therefore, I risked all and asked the boy to remove his jacket. I tore open the lining and, in the presence of the school doctor pulled out a plastic bag. The boy, white as a sheet, asked what I was going to do. I advised him to say nothing to anyone save his parents and the police. In his presence we telephoned his parents and told them the story; they then spoke to their son. I then contacted the police who immediately sent an officer to my study. We dismissed the boy informing him that we would see him as soon as we had a police report on the substance.

The policeman was as ignorant about drugs and cannabis as were the school doctor and I. We gazed at the package, which contained a greenish, slightly yellow flowery substance which certainly didn't look like resin but could well have been cannabis flowers. The policeman took charge of the package and said he would take it at once to the drug squad for analysis.

About three days later I received the report and relief was tinged with hilarity when I heard that the substance, which the boy had bought in Manchester for £30, was a mixture of shredded dried runner bean pods and curry powder.

We informed the parents and they agreed with me that the punishment should be that the school was informally alerted to the stupidity of their son.

I would take no further action as it was not against school rules to spend £30 of your money in the holidays on a package containing this particular mixture! The only comment that the boy made, shaking his head wearily, was 'I wondered why it didn't seem to give me a high!'

Little then did I realise what was in store for me a year later when I left Ellesmere having been invited to become the Head Master of Lancing College in Sussex.

HEAD MASTER

LANCING COLLEGE

1969 – 1981

❦

12

The First Term

WHENEVER we moved school we seemed destined not to be able to move into our house immediately. It had happened at Marlborough, where they were turning my bachelor quarters into a small married flat which was not completed until halfway through our first term so the College Porter very kindly lent us his retirement cottage. I did not find it easy to run a boarding house from there and be a new husband at the same time! At Ellesmere we could not move in because of the rewiring, and now, at Lancing, we could not move in because the house required redecoration. The College, however, did not at that time have much money and the Bursar explained to me that the redecoration could be completed neither by his staff nor by an outside contractor. He very kindly bought the paint and the brushes so that I could set to work with a will. For three weeks I painted the house while my wife and family stayed with her parents, with my mother arriving to alter curtains while I painted.

At the end of my first term we had decided we wished to change the dining room. I completed the last school report late one night just after term had ended, fetched a sledgehammer, knocked down a non-load-bearing temporary wall and went to bed. The following morning the dust had settled and the dining room had been extended! It was a lovely 16th century farmhouse and we were very spoilt to be able to live there. I still think it one of the best houses on the headmasters' circuit and it became a wonderful home in which our three children could have fun and grow up.

I knew when I accepted the invitation to become Head Master of Lancing College that my predecessor, Sir William Gladstone, had suceeded in making Lancing's housemasters more powerful and responsible within the management of the school. This made headmastering a fundamentally different exercise from my experience at Ellesmere. Gladstone had learned his trade as an assistant master and housemaster at Eton and brought with him to Lancing much of the style he learnt there as well as his inherent gentleness. The housemasters, therefore, had created their own house lists and entry to the school was healthy. He had continued Professor John Dancy's emphasis on the academic and so I inherited a stimulating and challenging Common Room.

The sixties were, however, not easy times, especially in the south of England, and some boys took advantage of Sir William's charm, especially when it came to appearance and length of hair. I knew that I had a problem to overcome in that area and Sir William readily acknowledged that this was so. His regime had been stimulating and gentlemanly; mine would have to be a little tougher, at least at the start. Incidentally, Sir William must be the only headmaster in history to become a Knight of the Garter.

One of Sir William's last decisions was to make the Prefects' Room a smoking area, with permission to smoke one of the privileges of being a Prefect.

During the holidays the connection between lung cancer and smoking was confirmed, so that one of my first tasks was to remove this privilege and this did not make me very popular. Another immediate difficulty which I inherited was that a boy the previous summer had brought cannabis into the school. If only it had been ground runner bean pods and curry powder! But it was not. Sir William dealt with the matter extremely well and firmly but, unfortunately, it hit the front pages of the national newspapers as Lancing became the first of the major independent schools to suffer from this partic- ular problem. That news, together with a feeling in the preparatory schools that Lancing might have become a little too liberal did not make recruitment easy. I felt that I had to be tougher than I might otherwise have been. I also was concerned lest it might be thought that I was not supportive enough of my predecessor; he certainly did not deserve the publicity which the school received in his final term.

The tradition at Lancing centres very much on the Chapel and around a long succession of old pupils who have distinguished themselves as play- wrights, actors and musicians. Both masters and pupils felt it was right that they should express themselves freely and fully and this was in great contrast to the previous school I had headmastered. It was something of an irony for me to have to play the more traditional authority figure as headmaster when I had for eight years at Ellesmere been doing the exact opposite!

Angela and I decided that when the parents brought back their offspring on the first day of term we would stand in the school library and receive them one by one. We began about 4.00 p.m. and did not finish until nearly 10.00 p.m. Exhausted, we returned home to find a splendid bottle of cham- pagne on the doorstep with a little note simply saying 'good luck!'

The real shock for me, however, was to receive well over 400 pupils with hair following the fashion of the day with exuberant enthusiasm. I recall one young man introduced to me, the son of a Royal Navy captain, of whom I could see nothing at all, as his hair, for 360 degrees, rested on his shoulders, front and back. His hands pulled the centrepiece apart to expose two very suspicious beady eyes. One glance at me was enough for him to drop his curtain and disappear! I realised that somehow or other I had to get some control over the hair in the school. The parents had lost control and they expected, quite unfairly, that the school would solve the problem. I talked with the housemasters about the problem and learnt that there was no school barber. A boy who wanted a haircut had to walk down to Shoreham-by-Sea and pay for it out of his pocket money. As none of them wanted their hair cut anyway I could see I was on a hiding to nothing if I continued with this scheme. Therefore, I appointed a school barber who was available, free of charge, on Wednesday afternoons between four and six. I placed a very small notice on the bottom of my noticeboard announcing this fact and hoped the housemasters would encourage pupils to go and get their hair cut so that it was at least off their collars. All headmasters at the time were fighting similar battles but it was a well-known fact that the Lancing boys had the longest hair.

All went pretty well and the housemasters were brilliant in supporting the plan. Nevertheless, the crunch came when one boy decided to lay his life on the line for his hair. He had quite beautiful wavy black hair, which flowed over his shoulders, rather like Charles the Second. He flatly refused to obey his housemaster, and his housemaster sent him to me. I requested that he had it trimmed. He refused. I asked him quite firmly to go and get it cut. He refused. I asked him what he would do if I ordered him to get it cut. He said he would decline.

We talked at length about the problem and he explained to me that during the holidays, and at exeat weekends, he mixed with another kind of society which expected his hair to be that length. 'Surely', he said, 'you would not want me to be ostracised by my friends at home?' 'Of course not', I replied, 'but this means that what we are really talking about is not the length of your hair but the kind of society that you wish to place first in your life. If you wish your education and your sixth form work to be top priority then, I fear, you must have your hair trimmed. But if you wish to put the holidays first then I fear you are in danger of opting out of this community and so losing your place in the school.' Today, this sounds rather harsh and it may well have been even then, but I could immediately recognise that I might be dealing here with the choice between academic discipline in a school and a possible group of drug-taking youngsters further along the Sussex coast.

The parents were extremely sympathetic. They wished very much to support the school. Indeed, they went so far as to produce a short-haired wig which he could wear while he was at school! Meanwhile, the entire community at Lancing was watching and waiting with bated breath. Who would win this battle? I knew jolly well that if I lost it I had lost the school and, whilst it might seem rather pathetic that I was making a crisis out of the length of one student's hair, it was clear to me that I had to push the situation to its logical conclusion. The boy left the school. Everyone else had their hair trimmed without a murmur or at least without a murmur to me.

I worried deeply about the boy after he left and was saddened, but not surprised, to hear that he had been arrested two weeks after leaving Lancing for possession of drugs. There followed a period of months and years when he moved from institution to institution. Each time he was free he came to see me at our house and we talked about his alternative society. He was very influenced by Woodstock (the site of the original 'love-in' in the USA in the sixties: flower power and drugs). I felt desperately sorry for him as he was so kind and intelligent.

About three years later he suddenly arrived at my front door one evening looking quite smart, totally aware of himself and carrying his form of application to go to university. Would I, he said, complete his UCCA form? I was, of course, delighted and he went on to gain a first-class degree and a fine job. I have not heard from him since but I know he became a teacher. I have not the slightest doubt that he will have been sensitive and sympathetic to all his pupils.

Hair continued to be a problem for many years and it was not until the eighties that Heads could begin to relax. Admittedly we had learnt a great deal about ourselves and relative priorities when it came to discipline. Honesty or dishonesty never altered but the width of boys' trousers certainly did. At Marlborough I was made to stand on the table at a housemasters' meeting to have the width of my trousers measured as it was thought I was a young man who was vaguely 'with it'. The school rule then became no tighter than my trousers. Ten years later, we were trying to stop th   going wider as the fashion had reverted to the twenties. Hair was similar and the young simply wanted to follow their heroes. I suppose we were all trying to break away from the conformity of war and 'short back and sides'. Indeed, one has only to look at photographs from that era to see that not only the boys, but parents and teachers also had untidy hair. The picture of HRH The Prince of Wales with the Head Master, tells all! Schools therefore became more tolerant places, restraining only extremes.

I only had one further problem with hair, much later at Harrow. Sometime before a visit by Her Majesty the Queen a housemaster telephoned me to say that a boy was demanding to see me as he objected to being sent home to have his hair re-dyed. It was shades of pink and green, as far as I can recall. The housemaster hoped that I would see the boy and support his decision. I saw the boy, informed him that his Housemaster's decision was a wise one, but then made a mistake, saying 'Anyway, Her Majesty The Queen is visiting and how could I possibly present you to her looking like that!' 'Oh, Sir,' he said, 'I stayed for three weeks with Prince Philip during the holidays and he had no objection at all.' Different schools need different policies.

During this time I also recall appointing a new master to teach in one of the academic departments at Lancing. Appointing new teachers is probably the most important single responsibility that falls on a head and I took a great deal of trouble about each appointment. Shortlisted candidates often stayed the night with us, were interviewed by my colleagues, met pupils and taught a lesson. On this particular occasion we had gone through all this procedure and I was finishing my acquaintance with the young man when I took him into the Lancing Chapel. The Chapel is the largest of its type in the world; it has the fourth highest nave and largest rose window of any church or cathedral in the United Kingdom. The Chapel itself and the worship and teaching which take place in it have a great effect on every pupil one way or another. I said to the young man I was interviewing 'and would you support what we are trying to do in this building?' 'Well, Head Master', he said, 'I think you could best call me a Woodstock man!' This episode epitomises some of the problems that headmasters were up against at that time. I said to the young man that I felt he should have done his homework a little more carefully before applying for a job in a school whose very foundation was for the purpose of teaching the Christian faith.

13

The Keys to the College

THE first term at Lancing went by very quickly and finished on a high note.
The boys went home at 11 am just after I had chaired a Masters' Common
Room meeting. Much earlier in the morning I had entered my study to find
on my desk a sealed envelope addressed to me. On opening it I found a visiting card from a group calling themselves 'The Silly Idiots Club' (SIC) with a
typed letter which read as follows:

Dear Mr Beer,

As you well know, many people do frivolous and unoriginal childish pranks on
their last night at School. We have decided that this practice should be altered. Thus
we have attempted to do something which we hope is original and certainly not
destructive. We have set out to show two things:

(1) That it is possible to get into a great many locked places in the School, and
(2) That it is possible to get to all these places unobserved and unchallenged.

We have visited the following places, and this can be confirmed by our visiting
cards, which we have left there:

Chemistry Preparation room	Record Library
Head of Chemistry's office	Armoury
Head of Physics's office	Arms cabinet
Technical centre	Strong Room
Physics preparation room	Accountant's office
Radioactive materials store	Main office
Hobbies room	Bursar's office
Chapel safe	Bursar's safe
High Altar	Petty cash box
High Altar (Crypt)	Head Master's study

This list does not cover our full range, but time is not infinite.

Yours sincerely,
S. I. C.

PS We apologize for the illiteracy, but as you will appreciate this was typed early in
the morning.

I was astonished as I realised that these boys had succeeded in entering every confidential area in the school. To their credit, when their letter was checked out, and all visiting cards were collected, no damage had been done and nothing had been stolen. I must say that I thought it a rather good wheeze until my door burst open and an extremely angry Bursar stormed into my study. Bill Tydd was an ex officer of the military police in Burma and I already knew by experience that he could become incandescent with rage. On this occasion he truly exploded and blamed the whole situation on me saying that he had felt for some time that I was not capable of controlling the boys in the school and that they were in his view out of control. I did my best to pacify him and promised him that I would get to the bottom of the matter and deal with it. In the meantime he insisted that every lock in the school would have to be changed and that the cost would be set against the Head Master's discretionary fund. By the time I had dealt with the Bursar it was time to go and chair the Common Room meeting.

Toward the end of the meeting, when general matters were being discussed, I asked, with as much innocence as I could summon, whether anyone had heard of the Silly Idiots Club. There was a silence until one young master said that he had found a card in the printing press which had been discarded by a senior boy. I asked the senior master to continue with the meeting while I took the young master outside with me. I showed him one of the visiting cards and he confirmed that it was identical to the one he had seen the boy discard, except that the discarded one was not well printed. He told me the name of the boy, who was a senior prefect and the son of the Vice-Chancellor of one of our major universities. I returned to the meeting, closed it down and had a word with the relevant housemaster who said he thought the boy had not yet left for his holiday. I asked him to send the boy to me at once.

The young man entered my study looking a little worried and rather surprised. I said to him 'Are you the guiding light in the Silly Idiots Club?' 'Yes, sir' he replied, 'Are you angry?' 'No, not at all', I said, 'it seems to me to be a very clever and, perhaps, constructive joke. However, what I want to know is how on earth you did it.' The story he then told me was extraordinary.

He had spent more than a month observing the Bursar. He had set up a watch through the windows into the Bursar's study. He had found that the Bursar had a routine which never varied. Apparently, at the end of the day, the Bursar would clear his desk, lock the petty cash box and place it in the main safe which contained all the keys to the rest of the school. He then locked the safe and placed the safe key in the top right-hand draw of his desk. He left his office on a self-locking latch with the key remaining on the inside.

The boys were aware of a tunnel which extended from the main school kitchens to the back of the Bursar's offices but was no longer used. It had originally been used to serve the masters in an era when part of what was now the Bursar's offices was the masters' dining room.

The boy had had gone through the tunnel and entered the Bursar's offices by placing newspaper under the door, poking the key through the door and dragging it under the door itself. He had then only to repeat performance at the Bursar's office door and he was in the inner sanctum. It was then an easy matter to extract the safe key from the Bursar desk, open the safe, borrow all the keys, and return to the kitchens. He had then spent a couple of hours leaving his visiting cards around the school before retracing his steps. It was his last term in the school as he had just sat his Oxbridge entrance exam. I wished him well for Christmas and for his future.

I knew that my meeting with the Bursar would be difficult. I left it until 'gin time' but he was understandably still deeply hurt by the whole episode, although he did agree not to change all the locks and not to charge anything to my discretionary account. I felt very sorry for him and, partly as a result of this episode, our friendship deepened.

He had the last laugh as the boys had another surprise for me at the end of my first year in office. On the morning that the boys were due to go home I drove from my house up the college drive to my study. At the top of the drive, between the Chapel crypt entrance and a boarding house on the other side of the drive, there was painted a superb zebra crossing. I had to stop to allow some boys across who had clearly been waiting for me. This time it was my turn to enter the Bursar's office and I asked him to have the offending zebra crossing removed before any parents arrived. He told me he thought it rather a good joke and that it would be impossible to remove it before the parents arrived, so that I would simply have to see the funny side and put up with it. I realised he had scored over me and I ignored the beastly crossing.

I had not, however, reckoned on my predecessor, Sir William Gladstone, arriving out of the blue. He came into my study, apologised for not warning me of his visit and hoped I did not mind. Of course I was delighted to see him and said so most enthusiastically. He asked me how I had been getting on and I told him of some of the problems, many of which he knew about and had indeed been wrestling with himself prior to his retirement. He then said what a brilliant idea of mine it was to create a zebra crossing from the Chapel across the drive. He could not understand why he had not thought of it himself and congratulated me! I feel guilty to this day that I never owned up to him that it was a joke played by the boys; I am sure he would have congratulated me on educating such intelligent and resourceful pupils.

14

The New Boys Project

PUPILS' careers are quite often modelled around their hobbies or spare time creative activities. I was therefore always concerned that a new boy coming into an independent secondary school might not have enough time to develop his creative talents. Today things are better with design and technology, art and music being compulsory in the curriculum, but even so a boy can so easily spend far too much time on the sports field and not enough time developing his God-given ability to create. I always made new boys make something in their first term outside of all school activities. This was easy to do in a boarding school and it also gave me the opportunity of getting to know each child through their creativity as well as forcing each boy to investigate the great variety of opportunities open to him in his spare time with the excellent facilities available. It became known as the New Boys Scheme and still exists in at least one of the schools I headmastered.

At the end of term I would hold an exhibition of all that they had made and was always astonished by the variety, expertise and endeavour displayed. Many of these creative works became Christmas presents, many were doubtless thrown away and one or two were given to me and remain precious objects to this day. I felt that sheer excellence needed some kind of recognition, and so at the prize-giving at the end of term I would give small book tokens to those who had achieved such distinction.

At the end of one winter term the whole school was assembled in the great hall at Lancing. I strode in and took centre stage whilst my colleagues were sitting in the gallery at the back of Hall. As a preamble to giving away achievement prizes for work, music and sport, as well as the new boys project achievement prizes, I addressed the school on some matter of importance before they went away on their Christmas holidays. As I addressed them I realised that there was an atmosphere of greater attentiveness than usual. Watching their eyes, it became apparent to me that something was attracting their attention just about the level of my head; certainly not my own eyes or my words. Slightly alarmed, and determined not to look up, I decided to give away one of the prizes before I had finished my main address.

I quickly selected a prize which I knew was to be given to a friendly pupil whom I could trust. I announced the award and the pupil walked up on to the platform. Having shaken him by the hand and congratulated him, I ventured to ask him what it was that everyone was looking at. He dismissed my question with disdain, 'The spider, of course', he said, and walked off the platform.

I went on addressing the school wondering what spider he was talking about and where it was. I decided to play to the gallery and risk all. Somehow I got into my speech some words concerning curds and whey and duly received a round of applause. Clearly, I was on the right track. I very slowly turned round to see it but could not and assumed that I had given it enough time to disappear. I decided to continue with my speech, and gave away the remaining prizes, finishing with a fictitious award to Miss Muffet and leaving the hall to a standing ovation.

Once outside the great hall, I quickly took one of the school prefects following me aside and asked him to explain exactly what was going on. He told me that one of the more creative sixth formers who was in the gallery (with the teachers!) had rigged up a length of wire down the hall, and fixed it around various pulleys until the end of the wire was over the centre of the stage. The young man had a lever in the gallery, which controlled the height of the wire above my head. On the end of the wire was a huge hairy spider about six feet across with superb eyes extending forwards on flexible springs. I was duly presented with this contraption and was thanked by the boy concerned for playing my part in the end of term proceedings 'correctly'. I breathed a sigh of relief and was grateful that my emphasis on creativity within the school seemed to be bearing fruit, although not quite of the sort I had anticipated.

It was now time for the pupils to go home and parents were gathering on the terraces outside the Chapel to collect their offspring. As usual, I went out to talk to individual parents and wish them well for the Christmas holidays. As I was talking to one set of new parents their young son joined them. Thankfully, I was able to remember exactly what he had made in the new boys project scheme. I praised the young man in front of his parents while he showed them the excellent piece of pottery he had made. At the same time, however, he said to his parents that his project was not nearly as good as the Head Master's. I was puzzled by this, as I had made nothing, but the parents, understandably, wanted to know what I had created. I was as curious as the parents were so I turned to the boy and said 'John, I think you had better tell your parents about my project'. The boy, full of excitement, began to tell his parents about the giant spider that I had made and had suspended above my head throughout the end of term proceedings. The boy was obviously greatly impressed and the parents turned to me to congratulate me. 'Ah, well . . .' I said, and hurried off quickly to meet some other parents while silently thanking that fine sixth form pupil and wondering whether I really had been dishonest: 'But Head Master, best to say nothing' I heard a voice within me saying . . .

On another occasion two of the new boys, William Caffyn and Robert Newton, succeeded in stuffing a fox. It was a very fine achievement for two thirteen-year-olds and I was much impressed. Trying to encourage them to aim even higher I said 'When you can stuff a frog then you will be real taxidermists' and thought no more about it. Five years later, just before they left Lancing to go to university, they arrived in my study with a leaving present for me. Inside a bell jar was a perfectly stuffed frog leaping through some small rushes which has been in my study ever since. They admitted it was not easy, for the epidermis of a frog is extremely thin and can easily tear. I asked them how many frogs they had killed to achieve their goal and I am sorry to say that they would not tell me, but I feared the worst. My conscience was very smitten when, two or three years later, I was summoned as the representative of the HMC to the Royal Society to discuss the shrinking frog populations and what we should do about it. At least the dissection of the frog was removed from the A-level syllabus.

14

The CCF and Sixth Form Lectures

I WAS often asked what was the main difference between being headmaster of Ellesmere College and Lancing College. One obvious difference was that the former played rugby football and the latter soccer as their main winter game. There is no doubt in my mind that this difference produced different physiques and different attitudes. Rugby football requires upper body strength whilst soccer, certainly at schoolboy level, requires greater agility and strength of the lower limbs. I could see that the way pupils who arrived at Ellesmere and Lancing at thirteen developed during adolescence directly reflected the winter game they were playing. I am not aware of any research into this but it would make a fascinating project. Certainly one of the great Victorian headmasters in the nineteenth century changed his main team game from soccer to rugby as he wanted his boys to have more exercise for their upper body.

Both schools were spoiled by visits from famous players. At Lancing, first or second division soccer teams would practice on the grounds and coach the boys in return. At Ellesmere I was able to bring Cardiff players to play annually with the boys, something that would not be allowed today. Boys such as Mark Keyworth and Bill Beaumont, both of whom went on to play for England, may well have been inspired by playing with, or watching, Gerald Davies, Gareth Edwards and others in that great Welsh back division of the seventies.

In my first year at Lancing the annual inspection of the Combined Cadet Force took place and the inspecting officer, whom I happened to know, arrived at my house for coffee. He asked me what was the biggest difference between the two schools and I took the CCF as an example. I said that both schools ran a very fine contingent, but if before the annual inspection took place the heavens opened, then I imagined that the Ellesmere CCF would stand still on the parade ground getting soaking wet and waiting with great determination for the inspecting officer to arrive. I imagined, on the other hand, that the Lancing CCF on feeling the first drops of rain would say to themselves, this is silly, let us go under cover, not get wet and wait for the inspecting officer. He laughed and we moved on to another topic.

While we were having our coffee, and unknown to us, the heavens had indeed suddenly opened and when we went to get into his car to drive to the inspection it was pouring with rain. He said nothing but my fingers were lightly crossed. We drove up the drive anticipating the great sight of the Lancing CCF lined up on the parade ground. There was no one to be seen. A young sergeant ran out from the Chapel cloister, saluted smartly and said 'Sir, we thought it silly to stand in the rain and get wet, and so we have lined up under cover in the Chapel cloister and are ready for your inspection!' The inspecting officer was vastly amused. Neither of us commented on which was the better approach.

Lancing's originality never ceased to surprise me and the boys were always trying to get 'one up' on the authority of the school. Indeed, I found it became quite a personal battle between the sixth form and myself but always in the friendliest way. I was in the habit at the beginning of the school term of mentioning any good news which might have happened during the holidays. On one occasion, about two days before term began I had received a letter from a member of the general public who lived in Yorkshire about the behaviour of our skiing party that January. The letter emphasised that they were the liveliest group of young men that this man and his wife had ever met and, indeed, they did make a certain amount of noise. The letter went on to emphasise, however, that they always knew where to draw the line, always apologised if they had 'gone over the top' and altogether made a deep impression for good on this couple. As this is not always true of school skiing parties, I decided to quote a part of the letter to the school. When I got to that part of my address, I found that I had left the letter behind in my study. I therefore apologised to the school and simply said that I was pleased to have received the letter. I thought no more about it until at lunchtime one of the senior boys, Timothy Horne, said 'It is not easy to fool you is it?' I had no idea what he was talking about and so accepted the compliment and gently probed. It turned out that he had been on the skiing party and that he had been the author of the letter and posted it in Yorkshire; but he had also been convinced that I had seen through his ruse by leaving the letter behind in my study. Not for the first time did I fail to disabuse him.

This episode was in great contrast to a skiing party from Harrow during my time as Head Master there. I received a letter from an elderly couple who complained that the boys had been far too rowdy when a birthday party for one of the boys had wrecked his wife's enjoyment of the evening. I wrote and apologised, and although they lived a long way away, invited them to lunch so that they could meet some Harrovians and, I hoped, discover that they could be very polite and extremely good company. Rather to my astonishment the couple accepted the invitation and my wife and I arranged for the main perpetrator of the noise to be present at the lunch. He performed his task brilliantly, realising why our guests had been invited, apologising with great aplomb and taking them off for coffee in his study. Young people rarely let you down and the school made two good friends that day.

On another occasion when I was addressing the whole school at Lancing at the end of term the boys decided it would be a brilliant idea if I were to disappear in a cloud of dry ice. I learned afterwards that they had spent a great deal of money on the equipment but fortunately heard some noises behind me on the stage and, without realising what I was doing, saved myself by frightening the operator away.

I was not always so fortunate. I had invited my brother, Professor Stafford Beer, to visit the college and address the sixth form on cybernetics. His appearance, in traditional public school terms, left something to be desired. He attended Chapel in his poncho and beads whilst his beard, which stretched to his navel, caused particular merriment amongst the fifth formers. I knew this was likely to happen and had therefore introduced him on the school calendar not as Professor Stafford Beer but as the President of the World Cybernetic Society.

Unfortunately, that very day I had a serious problem to resolve involving a clash of the sort that sometimes occurred at Lancing and indeed other schools between the enthusiastic anglo-catholic and the equally enthusiastic evangelical masters. They had allowed their differences of opinion concerning worship to develop into open conflict. The question of the number of candles on the altar, the use of incense or of prayer meetings in people's rooms appeared to have become more important than the heart of the matter, a belief in Jesus Christ as the Son of God. I therefore summoned all the parties involved into my study to try to sort the issues out. On that occasion I decided not to have a discussion but simply to tell them all to get their priorities right and behave. I did not allow anyone to sit down and they realised at once that I was upset and angry. I told them all exactly what I thought and pulled no punches. There was a stunned and embarrassed silence. At that precise moment my brother chose to open the door, uninvited and unheralded, and say 'Well, have you sorted this lot out yet?' I wished the ground could have swallowed me up until I heard my colleagues roaring with laughter. From that moment we were all united and I had no further worries on that particular aspect of worship at Lancing. The only person in the room who did not understand the laughter was my brother.

He gave a brilliant talk to the sixth form, as I knew he would, and captivated his audience. He finished by presenting them with an extremely complex problem saying 'If any of you can solve this problem the Head Master will give you a case of claret!' Needless to say this caused quite a stir, and not only with me. It was a popular gesture at the expense of the Head Master. As I thanked him publicly I thought this was the moment to lift the veil and claim the President of the World Cybernetic Society as my elder brother. Amazingly, the captain of the school, Michael Weir, solved the problem, received the prize and went on to read cybernetics at Reading University.

This lecture was one of a series which we held for the sixth form every Wednesday afternoon. The lecturers usually dined with us in the evening and stayed the night. I was always looking for good lecturers and one of my chemistry staff, Dr Robert Peck, informed me that there was a brilliant scientist, Professor David Phillips, in the Biochemistry Department at Oxford University who would be first class on RNA and DNA. I wrote to him and invited him to visit Lancing. He readily accepted. He duly arrived and I introduced him to the sixth form and the Masters. As he began his lecture I received a note passed to me by Dr Peck. The note said 'This is not Professor Phillips. I have no idea who he is.' I was a trifle shaken but as the lecture was excellent I tried to put the information out of my mind. At the end I thanked him, asked the sixth form to look after him for an hour and then to bring him to our house for pre-dinner drinks.

Outside the lecture room I immediately accosted Robert Peck. He again stoutly denied that this was Professor Phillips. 'After all', he said, 'Professor Phillips was my tutor for my PhD and I knew him well.' I said to the young man, with some determination, that, as he was dining with Professor Phillips that evening, would he please pretend to be the Professor's old pupil to save us all embarrassment? He eventually agreed.

Professor Phillips arrived and I explained to him who was coming to dinner, and that amongst their number would be his old pupil Dr Peck. 'Dr who?' he said. 'You remember,' I said 'Robert Peck, who took his PhD under your tutelage.' 'Oh, yes, yes I think I remember him. It will be good to meet him again!'

When Dr Robert Peck entered the dining room I introduced him to the Professor as his old pupil and the two of them acted their parts with complete aplomb.

When Professor Phillips left I did some urgent research and found to my astonishment that connected with the Biochemistry Department at the University of Oxford there were two Professor David Phillipses, both of them capable of delivering brilliant lectures. Dr Peck's tutor I never met; the Professor I entertained was, amazingly, born in Ellesmere, had attended the primary school in the town and assumed that I had invited him for that reason. He never found out about the mistake. He later became Lord Phillips of Ellesmere but, sadly, is now dead.

Lancing, 13 May 1978. Bishops process to meet the Archbishop of Canterbury.

ancing. HRH Prince Charles walks to his helicopter having opened the first girls' house and attended
Sung Eucharist. Lavinia, Duchess of Norfolk, the Lord Lieutenant, walks immediately behind.

Lancing, 13 May 1978. The dedication of the new rose window. HRH Prince Charles and the author lead out the procession.

Lancing, July 1981. The author and Mrs Beer say farewell to pupils and parents outside the Crypt after their final Sung Eucharist.

Philip, Caroline and Martin opening their Grandmother's Christmas present in the new house at Harrow, 1983

Harrow, 28 January 1983. Lady Soames DBE, younger daughter of Winston Churchill, and Mr Geoffrey Simmonds, Old Harrovian, at the opening of the Sixth Form Club. At the time Lady Soames was the only woman Governor and Geoffrey Simmonds the American Governor of Harrow

Tim Wilkinson, Custos of Harrow School, friend and adviser to young and old alike.

Harrow, November 1983. The opening of the new photographic studio by Lord Lichfield (*left*). Also pictured are the author (*centre*) and Richard Shymansky, the school photographer, who has since moved his studio to Eton.

Churchill Songs on 2 December 1983. The Prime Minister and Mr Denis Thatcher with the Monitors

February 1985. 100th anniversary celebration of the Eton-Harrow fives competition.
Left to right: Dr Eric Anderson, Headmaster of Eton, Lord Charteris, the author and Lord Home.

Harrow, 19 November 1985. The inauguration of the Shaftesbury Lecture on the centenary of the death of the 7th Earl of Shaftesbury, Anthony Ashley Cooper. HRH the Queen Mother presents her portrait to the school.

Harrow, 24 November 1986. Visit of Her Majesty the Queen and HRH the Duke of Edinburgh. Inspecting the Guard of Honour.

The resurrection of the Silver Arrow competitio[n] The Mayor and Mayores[s] of Harrow with Mrs Angela Beer.

January 1987. Fund raisi[ng] party at 10 Downing Str[eet] hosted by the Prime Minister and Mr Denis Thatcher. *Left to right*: James Stoney, Anstrumann Woodhull, the first Malaysian to be Head of School, the author, Jocelin Ings-Chambers.

14

The Amazing Shooting Incident

ON one occasion we invited the author Tom Sharpe, a former Lancing pupil, to give a Wednesday afternoon lecture. The opening line of his lecture made his listeners sit up faster than any other I had ever heard. He started with the words 'Hands up those of you who were buggered at your prep school'! The rest of his talk was an improvement on the opening sentence and the evening dinner party was one of the most amusing we had ever held. His conversation became racier and racier, whilst his wonderful wife insisted that he was not really a vulgar man. He was huge fun. The following story could have come straight out of a Tom Sharp novel but is actually true.

Angela and I were returning from a party early one evening in the summer term. We arrived at the top of the College drive to be told that there had been some trouble during prep involving some of the local youths who were advancing from the masters' houses on the far part of the College estate and that Mr Jeremy McLachlan had sent for the police. I was much concerned as we had had some difficulties with the young of Lancing town and some of them had been coming up to the College buildings and throwing stones at the windows. I therefore turned the car round and drove back onto the main road and up towards the masters' houses. I left Angela in the car and began to walk across the field with Mr McLachlan. He explained his concerns to me and we proceeded across the field towards the College. At that moment we heard explosions which caused us to stop and Mr McLachlan to exclaim 'They are firing guns at us!' Desperately trying to calm everything down I said 'Don't be silly, no one would do that, they are fireworks or thunderflashes.' Little did I realise then just how wrong I was. It was agreed that the matter should be left in my hands and I would go to the College and sort it out.

I returned with Angela in the car as fast as I could and drove to the top end of the College buildings where I thought the problem was centred. Some very excited senior boys were there who told us that the local youths had gone away. One then said, 'Jolly well had to after we fired at them!' One of the others told him to shut up but it was too late. I immediately interrogated the young man who claimed that some boys from a particular House had fired shotguns. I drove at once to the boarding house concerned, went in and asked for the housemaster. I was told that both he and the tutor were out to dinner and that the head of house was in charge.

I asked the head of house what was going on and he informed me that two boys had fired shotguns at local youths. I confiscated the guns and spoke to the two boys concerned. I was angry and worried and told them to say nothing to anyone, remain in their studies until further notice, and warned them that they were in serious trouble. We returned to our house, with the guns, and wondered what on earth was going on. At that moment the telephone rang and the father of one of the boys asked me whether it was true that his son was in trouble. I told him that it was, and explained that shotguns had been fired. The father replied that *he* was aware of this, but was *I* aware who had given the orders? I immediately sensed trouble and said that I was not. He then told me that the housemaster, before leaving for his dinner party, had said 'and if any of the local 'yobs' come near the House let off a few salvos over their heads.' The father asked me what was my reaction. I thanked him and said I was looking into the matter and would report further. I simply could not believe what I was being told.

After I had calmed down, I saw the boys again and asked for the full story. It turned out that they had brought the shotguns back to school from home. The housemaster had not declared them to anyone but had kept them in his House. Indeed, some of the cartridges had had the lead shot removed by the housemaster's wife, with the help of the boys, and rice had been substituted. As the boys had been told by their housemaster to use the guns should the local youths appear, they had taken the guns from their storage place and fired them off over the heads of the local youths, using the 'rice' cartridges. They had then fired a lead cartridge as well. No one had been hurt. Again I restricted them to their studies to await further instructions. I requested that the head of house ask the housemaster to come to my house the moment he returned from the dinner party.

He duly came and when confronted with the story, as related to me by the boys, denied nothing. I immediately relieved him of his duties as housemaster and said we would take the matter further in the morning. I then telephoned the Chief Constable of West Sussex, gave him all the facts, told him of my action but emphasised that I was deeply concerned lest the local youths should feel inclined to retaliate. He expressed appreciation that I had informed him at once and told me he would discuss the problem with the local police in order to prevent any escalation of violence.

The next morning my worst fears were realised: the local newspaper was on the telephone. The reporter had all the facts correctly presented and he wanted my comments prior to publication. I simply asked that he should see his Editor and ask him to telephone the Chief Constable immediately. The reporter was amazed that the Chief Constable should know of the incident. I said no more but beseeched him to take the matter to his highest authority as I had done. To its eternal credit, the newspaper never published a word, as they were as concerned as the Chief Constable and I that there should be no escalation of violence between the local young and the young of the College. As far as I am aware the story never reached the national press. The local youths did not return and peace once again reigned.

The housemaster was one of the most efficient administrators that I had ever worked with and had been a genius with the organisation of the timetable in his time. He stayed for a further few terms at Lancing but was then appointed headmaster of another school and with him went this astonishing story.

It put me in mind of another shooting incident in which I was involved as a very young master at Marlborough College. In those days a small group of masters used to go out rough shooting when we had a spare afternoon. Normally we took a few boys from the junior house to act as beaters. On one occasion my friend and colleague, Dennis Silk (later Warden of Radley College) was in the group together with the school doctor, Dr Tommy Hunter, and a senior housemaster, Leslie Coggin. Dennis and I had asked for volunteers for beaters from our two Houses and we had about four boys. All went well until a pheasant rose in front of us and Leslie Coggin let fly with one barrel. He hit the bird, which fell in front of us into a hedge. We were all very excited as he was not, normally, a good shot and had not 'bagged' a bird for many months, possibly years. Unknown to us, the boys acting as beaters, also very excited, rushed round to the back of the hedge, which we could not see, in order to retrieve the bird. When they tried to grasp the pheasant it rose once more, and Leslie, seeing his bird disappearing, let fly with the other barrel. This time he was not nearly so accurate. We heard an agonised cry behind the hedge and, rushing around to see what had happened, discovered a boy lying down with shot marks on his thigh and the others standing around pointing at him saying 'They've shot Byers!'

We were fortunate to have the doctor in our party. The boy was taken away and had lead shot removed from his thigh. Fortunately, it had not gone any higher and it was clear he would recover fully. Nevertheless, parents had to be informed, as well as the Master, for the matter was obviously delicate. The young man lived in Africa and we had to send a telegram to the parents explaining all. By return we received a telegram from the parents 'Very sorry to hear about Robin. Please keep us informed but very much hope that this incident will not prevent him from being accepted as a beater in future.' I have a horrid feeling that today the reaction of parents might be rather different and I dread to think how the media would have reacted.

I watched Byers as he went up the school. He became a very good sprinter and an excellent cellist. I recall he told me on one occasion that lead shot appeared every now and again by his knee joint. Pieces came to the surface and were removed. I did not see him again until I was Head Master of Harrow when he appeared as the godfather to one of the Harrow boys at a confirmation service. My wife, who had always doubted my story, had it confirmed that day. The grown-up Mr Byers was every bit as charming and understanding as he was as a boy—with lead shot still occasionally coming to the surface.

17

MI6

N o r has this story ever been recorded.

I was sitting by my desk in my study at Lancing late one morning when my secretary told me that there was someone on the telephone wanting to speak to me who would not give his name. I took the call and heard a voice asking whether I was on my own as the matter he wanted to discuss was confidential. I assured him that no one else was present and he then asked if he could see me in my house that evening at 6 p.m. if that would be convenient to me. Needless to say, I asked him who he was and he said simply that it was a matter of national security. I assumed, quite wrongly, that it was another visit by security people to carry out the vetting procedure on an old Lancing pupil who was to be given some sensitive role. Far from it.

At 6 p.m. precisely the front doorbell rang and outside were two gentleman who immediately produced their identity cards indicating that they were from MI6. They came into my drawing-room and asked if conversation there could be overheard. I felt like looking behind all the curtains before we began, but resisted the temptation and informed them all was well. They then asked me if I had a certain pupil in the school and gave me his name. I said that I had. They then asked me what I knew about him and I responded by demanding to know what was their business. They explained that they had reason to believe that the young man concerned, who had only been in the school one year, was in the sixth form and came from the Middle East, was connected with a plot to blow up an aeroplane at Heathrow. I could hardly believe what I was hearing and asked for some more detail. This they refused to give me except to state quite categorically that they had reason to believe that an aeroplane might be blown up and they asked me whether the young man concerned had been in London during certain dates. The dates they gave me coincided with weekend exeats from Lancing and so I told them it was quite possible. I was asked whether I knew who his friends were in London and I had to confess ignorance.

They then made the most extraordinary request I have ever had made of me. They asked me to steam open his letters, read them and inform them of anything which might have a bearing on what they were investigating. My immediate reaction was to tell them that I could not possibly carry out their request. They sat in silence and looked at me and then said 'Head Master, if 350 people are killed in an aeroplane on the tarmac at Heathrow it will be partly on your conscience.' I thought that a little unfair and we continued our discussion until I told them that I would think about it and let them know the following morning. Of course, I could talk to no one, but rightly or wrongly, I came to the conclusion that if I did steam open the letters and there was nothing in them I would help to prove the young man's innocence. If I did not open them and anything happened, then, as they had said, it would be on my conscience. I knew that whatever I did it would be on my conscience . . .

So I steamed open the letters but we found nothing and I reported this to my authority.

The following week the young man concerned asked his housemaster whether a friend of his could stay at the weekend as he had not seen him for some time. The housemaster, Ted Maidment, later a very distinguished Headmaster of Shrewsbury School, came to see me to ask whether this would be in order as he knew that I was concerned about this particular boy, although he did not know why. I gave approval on the condition that he recorded the visitor's name, the number of his passport, his date of birth, the country he had flown from including the airline and flight number and where he was going next. Ted Maidment looked at me in amazement and began to ask me questions. 'No questions, please,' I said and he left.

On Monday morning Ted came to see me and gave me all the relevant information. I thanked him and waited. Sometime in the afternoon MI6 telephoned and asked to see me in my house that evening. This time they asked me if I knew the name of a young man who had, apparently, stayed the weekend at Lancing. I told them I did, asked them to open their notebooks and gave them all the information. 'Head Master,' one of them said 'would you like to be an honorary member of MI6?'

The following week I switched on our television set to see an aeroplane on the runway at Heathrow airport and announcements that tanks were surrounding the airport. No aircraft was blown up and all was well although the event was headline news in all the national media.

I contacted my two 'colleagues' and asked them to give me a report on my pupil. They informed me that as far as they were concerned he was totally innocent but that it would be wise for me to have a private word with him, suggesting that he should be more careful about the company that he kept when he visited London. I did that and the young man concerned expressed his gratitude. For my part I wondered why such problems did not feature on headmasters' training courses!

Curiously, there was a follow-up to this particular saga and I began to become a little worried lest security forces were keeping a particularly close eye on the pupils. A highly intelligent lower sixth former, whilst in Brighton, bought an extreme left-wing newspaper from a young man on the streets as he was curious to see what it contained. I was somewhat alarmed when I was visited, once more, by security officers who wanted full details of the boy's background and whether I thought that he was a revolutionary. This time I became a trifle angry and refused. I think they understood and I heard no more from them.

Instead, it became my turn to be 'got at' by security officials. A sixth form pupil arranged to travel during his gap year to South Africa, meet his aunt in Cape Town and then go on to teach in a black school. He went by boat to Cape Town, was detained on board, not allowed to see his aunt, taken by police car to the airport and deported back to London. On arrival in London he came down to see me to ask what was going on and what could I do about it. I promised to look into the whole matter as quickly as I could. I contacted a friend of mine, Gordon Waddell, who had played rugby for Cambridge and Scotland and was in the South African parliament, but he simply told me that it would be a waste of his and my time to ask questions. We would get nowhere. I therefore began my investigations in England. I found that an article had been written in the boy's local newspaper mentioning the fact that he had been helped by Bishop Winter in Oxford. Bishop Winter had been deported from South Africa and it seemed clear to me that this was the reason why this young man was also *persona non grata*.

It seemed to me tragic that this eighteen-year-old should be turned against the whole of the South African regime as a result of its own stupid actions. He had gone out there with an open mind, but now he began to work voluntarily against apartheid. I decided to write to *The Times* newspaper giving the simple facts and asking why it was that a nation could behave in such a petty way towards a totally innocent and open-minded sixth former who only wanted to teach black children in South Africa. My letter was not acknowledged by *The Times*. In my experience, this was most unusual. Many weeks later the letter suddenly appeared. I can only assume that it was being vetted by someone along the line. There followed some anonymous telephone calls from rather aggressive sounding gentlemen with guttural voices, telling me to mind my own business or else . . .

I had been invited to speak on two occasions in South Africa but had declined as I was opposed to apartheid. I was known to be the lone voice on the Rugby Football Union Committee opposing the England rugby team going there, although eventually the Committee was unanimous in opposing tours to South Africa. But when I heard that my colleagues in the independent schools in South Africa, despite accepting children from all races and creeds, were being given financial support by the government, I decided to go. I went out to address their Headmasters Conference and Governors Association to give them support and advise them on the setting up of an Independent Schools Council to deal with the government. My next visit was with the England rugby team in 1994, three weeks after Mandela had been elected President, and I spent a happy afternoon with him in Pretoria. Bishop Trevor Huddlestone, who had been expelled from South Africa for opposing apartheid and had himself been a boy at Lancing, had helped Oliver Tambo's son to come to Lancing College under my headship. President Mandela and I therefore had something to talk about other than rugby football, about which he understandably knew little.

18

Endless Pranks

MAYBE it was something in the sea air, but in no other school in which I have served have I experienced so many practical jokes of one kind or another as I did at Lancing. Shortly after arriving there, and still in the mode of visiting as many parts of the college as possible, I unearthed a beer making factory under the drain covers of the chapel. Under the covers let into the ground, below the drainpipes, were small pits into which pupils had inserted dustbins full of fermenting beer. I simply poured the beer down the drain. To this day, I have no idea who was the brewer or what they did when they found their fermenting wort had gone!

There was a long tradition at Lancing of having fun on the night before speech day or the last night of term. After twelve years as Head Master these two particular times did begin to wear me down. I found those were the only nights when I could not sleep very well.

I recall one occasion, at the end of the summer term, having to get out of bed at about 2 a.m. as I could hear voices from afar. I put on my dressing gown and slippers and walked outside to listen in the still air for the voices, which seemed to me to come from the direction of the tuck shop, about 400 yards from our house. I walked slowly up the drive to see what was going on. At that time of a summer morning voices carry a long way and I was drawn further and further away from the house, feeling more and more stupid in my nightshirt, dressing gown and slippers. There were no boys near the shop and so I wandered across the playing fields attracted as a moth to the light by the raucous laughter and happy screams of young people having fun. I traversed the upper fields, and then the lower field, and then the copse until I was overlooking the estuary of the river Adur. Just below me I could see in the moonlight a fairly large group of boys clearly enjoying themselves. Some were in rubber dinghies, some in canoes, others in small rowing boats and sailing boats. Some, by their movements, looked as if they might have had a little too much to drink. I stood and watched, realising just how stupid I would look. Fortunately, I had been wise enough to take a large torch with me and so, switching it on and shining it down onto the river, I shouted in as

big a 'blue' voice as I could 'The Police! What are you doing?' I knew that if I
kept the torch shining they would not be able to see me, but it was hardly
necessary as I have seldom seen a group disperse so rapidly in my life. They
jumped into the water, they splashed, they swam, they pulled the boats to
the shoreline and began to run up towards the College. I had the advantage
of being able to take a shortcut across the field and was able to intercept a
small group at the back of this crowd of lemmings as they rushed toward the
dormitories.

In the dark I quietly walked up to the last three and said softly 'Excuse me
but it is the Head Master here. What have you been doing and why are you
all out of bed?' They nearly jumped out of their skins, which gave me some
satisfaction. I almost felt that I might not look quite so stupid in my night
clothes after all. Of course, I knew their names and their housemasters. I told
them that I would hold them personally responsible for any misbehaviour
from that moment onwards until the pupils returned home with their parents at the end of term. If the school behaved well then I would forget what
and whom I had seen.

I returned to our house and slept easily knowing that the end of term
would be peaceful. I was not mistaken. The following day, however, I ran
into one of my prefects who had broken his leg. As the previous day he had
looked perfectly all right I inquired how he had succeeded in breaking it. He
said that he had fallen down the stairs in his boarding house and been taken
to hospital that morning. I commiserated with him and told him how sorry
I was. I learnt, several years later, that whilst the latter was true the former
was not. He had, in fact, rushed away from the river Adur so fast that he had
slipped on the bank and fallen. He was the only casualty of that particular
evening as far as I know.

I had long had a connection with educational organisations in the USA
which arranged for pupils to be exchanged between the UK and USA. I was
therefore not surprised when, during the summer holidays between leaving Ellesmere and arriving at Lancing, I received an urgent call asking
whether I would accept a young man into Lancing in the September. It was
difficult for me as the housemasters had not yet met me and I was not sure
how they would react to this sudden addition of a senior pupil from abroad.
Fortunately, I knew that Ken Shearwood, one of the housemasters, might
be interested and I was able to contact him and persuade him to accept the
boy.

The boy, when I met him, turned out to be slightly more mature than
most of the junior masters. He was about six-foot-four, weighing in at about
fourteen stone, extremely well built and with a huge shock of curly red hair.

He was remarkably talented: intelligent, a good writer, a good talker and a good sportsman. He made an immediate impact on the sixth form and, to begin with, the influence was all for the good. He was very quickly selected as a member of the English Speaking Union debating team for the College and helped us to win locally, regionally and then to appear in the final in London.

The team planned to leave Lancing by the early train but breakfast came and there was no sign of Jim Austin. He had simply disappeared and when more questions were asked it became apparent that he had not been in his room the previous night. Someone said they thought he had gone to do some research at the University of Sussex. We contacted the university and he was eventually found, fast asleep, in the university library. By this time the other members of the team had travelled to London and Jim Austin was ordered by the university to report to the Head Master of Lancing immediately. By the time he arrived in my study I was very angry as it looked as if he had been out all night and possibly denied us a national trophy. I gave him a piece of my mind. I told him a taxi awaited him outside, that he would go immediately to London and that he would be paying the bill. He only made one remark. 'Gee', he said 'I have never seen a man so angry in all my life!' We won, but that was not the end of the story of Mr Jim Austin.

He had not only succeeded with the debating team but he was also succeeding on the tennis courts and helped the team to get through to the final at junior Wimbledon. It was the first time that Lancing had appeared in such a final. It was also the first time that Lancing had a man ordered off the court at the home of tennis. He came home in disgrace muttering 'Gee whiz, what a silly umpire!'

I only saw him once again, when I was on a lecture tour in America with my wife. Very charmingly he arranged to meet us in New York. He was determined to take us out to dinner at one of his favourite restaurants. We had an extremely amusing evening: it was the first and last time Angela and I took a 'doggy bag' home full of T-bone steak. He was a fine host and by this time was doing well at university. Just before the bill came, he was called away for an urgent telephone call leaving me to settle the account. Somehow he managed to pass this sort of thing off and today he is probably a highly successful businessmen, politician or lawyer.

The Directorship of Music at Lancing is not an easy job as in addition to all the normal duties it involves choosing and inspiring all the music sung in the great Chapel. During my career I do not think I made many mistakes in appointing masters. There was, however, one Director of Music whom I should not have appointed. Not because he was not a fine musician, for he was certainly that, but because he really did not understand the deeper anglo-catholic ethos of the school. He was of a much more evangelical persuasion and, whilst he knew the background history of the school, felt that he would be able to adapt. Things began to go wrong when he decided to create a supplement to our hymn book. We used the *English Hymnal* but he felt that we should be singing many more modern hymns. He therefore created a supplement which contained a different set of hymns which the boys were expected to sing. Boys, however, can be the most reactionary people on God's earth, even during the 1970s. The supplement was a small ringbound folder so that new hymns could be slipped in quite easily. Needless to say, hymns already in the supplement could equally easily be slipped out. The night before the service when one of these hymns was due to be sung a boy, or boys, crept into chapel and removed the appropriate sheet from each supplement. This direct action was highly effective, for how could 450 boys be expected to sing when they had no words in front of them? The sheets were all put back properly the following night. The Director of Music began to get the message and retired, but the reaction of the boys was, for me, typically Lancing and not all that easy to handle.

One morning two boys, Alexander Luce and Stephen Robinson, came to see me in my study to ask if they could go on a water diet for three days to raise money for the starving in the Third World. They presented the idea to me as a challenge, which clearly meant that I should be setting a good example as well. The outcome was more dramatic than I expected as all three of us had to secure medical permission, permission from parents and housemasters and, in my case, from my wife. It was an interesting experience and I was told that during the final part of the third day I was sufficiently light-headed for colleagues to be attempting to get permission to do all kinds of things, including spending money, which they would normally never have dreamed of trying on. We raised a good sum and I lost more weight than I had expected. The curious thing was that I did not really want to eat on the fourth day and, for the first time really began to understand the feelings of an anorexic boy whom we were trying to help at that time. I am glad to say that he eventually gained an Exhibition to Oxford.

I had been at Lancing for over ten years when one morning I opened a letter from the Provost of Eton asking me if I would meet the Fellows concerning a vacancy for the headmastership which was about to arise. I was flattered, slightly frightened and wondered whether it would be the right move for me. The next letter I opened was an almost identical one from Harrow. A left and right in one post. I was bowled over and knew there would be some difficult decisions ahead.

In the end I decided to meet both sets of governors. Lord Charteris, the then Provost of Eton, said 'my enthusiasm would be admirably suited to Harrow', whilst Harrow invited me to become their Head Master. I hesitated, as I was not very keen on leading a traditional school which might not be prepared to accept change. After all I was a biologist who believed in evolution. I expressed my concern to the governors and also told them that I was concerned about the Head Master's living accommodation at the school. Traditionally the Head Master's house was not only his office but had been a boarding house for about ninety boys controlled by him. In more recent years the governors had realised that this was too much of a strain on the Head Master and had handed the responsibility of the boarding house over to a resident housemaster. However, the Head Master continued to live with his family in the centre of the house, where he also had his office. The housemaster and his family lived in accommodation attached on one side.

At Lancing we were living in a wonderful 16th century farmhouse and I was not prepared to uproot Angela and the three children to live in such different conditions at Harrow. I expressed my concern and returned home believing that we were not destined to lead Harrow School after all. I had not reckoned on a very lively and young governing body who, I learnt later, held private meetings in which they came to the conclusion that, whoever became the new Head Master, he and his family would live in a new house away from his office and the boarding house. The new Head Master would then decide where his office should be. Various suggestions were made, although I eventually decided that it was best for the office to be in the centre of the school at the very top of Harrow Hill where it had traditionally been for centuries.

Several months after my original interview, I was visited by Mr Donald Lindsay who had previously been Headmaster of Malvern College, Chairman of the Headmasters' Conference and was then the masters' governor at Harrow School. He had been sent to tell me that a new house would be built and, in these circumstances, would I consider being the Head Master. I decided to meet with the governing body for a second time and, encouraged by their plan of action for the Head Master's house, decided to ask them, once again, about change at Harrow. They told me that they had come to the conclusion that in 1981 they wanted change. I asked them what it was that I could change at Harrow. The answer I received cleared my mind and made me accept the invitation. 'Headmaster, I think you can change anything at Harrow but for goodness sake don't try and change anything unimportant!' And so it came about that I found myself, after 12 years, walking down the Chapel at Lancing to preach my last sermon to the school on the final day of the summer term 1981. As I climbed the steps into the pulpit I saw that there was a note for me on the lectern. In order to understand the meaning of the message it is necessary to go back twelve years to when I addressed the new boys on their first day at Lancing. Partly because of my experience at Ellesmere with boys running away, and partly because I was concerned about the proximity of Brighton, I said to them that if they ever felt unhappy and wanted to run away home, they must do so. But, as they would have to pass my house at the bottom of the College drive on the way out, would they please call in so that my wife or I could give them a bottle of coke and some sandwiches to see them on their way. No one ever did. Run away, that is!

The message on the pulpit lectern read 'Look down at your feet. Goodbye.' I looked down at my feet and there in the pulpit by my feet was a bottle of coke and some sandwiches. I could hardly get out the first sentence of my sermon.

HEAD MASTER

HARROW SCHOOL

1981 – 1991

❧❧❧

19

The Start

ONCE again, it was not possible to move into our private house for the family as it was still being built. We therefore lived in the old Head Master's flat in the Head Master's boarding house. I knew that leading Harrow would be a different experience from anything I had met before and so it proved. It was more like conducting an orchestra and therefore very important to bring in the right people at the right time. I found the whole experience very stimulating, but I had still not learnt not to take early decisions and found that I was changing things even before term began.

It had been the custom for new boys to arrive with their parents in the early evening on the first day of term. They were welcomed by their housemasters and given tea, following which the parents had sherry with the housemaster privately. The Head Master did not feature at all. I suggested to the housemasters that, after they had given the parents sherry, they should invite them to go to the Speech Room to be welcomed by the Head Master. Several of the housemasters were suspicious and wondered what I was going to do. They asked me what I wanted to say to the parents and I simply told them that if I were sending a boy to any school I would wish to meet the Head Master, particularly if he was new. They accepted this, the plan was put into operation and I became the first modern Harrow Head Master to address all new parents on the first day of term. Quite a few parents who were not new to Harrow got wind that the new Head Master was going to speak in the Speech Room and the place was packed with parents of all years.

My wife and I walked up to the Speech Room to meet the Custodian of the School, a very important figure, who was welcoming parents in his morning coat and showing them to their seats. He met the two of us outside Speech Room and quietly asked us if I was ready to go in. I was absolutely petrified but would have been no more ready if we had waited a further thirty minutes. At that moment an extremely attractive lady walked past us into the Speech Room. Custos said 'If I were you, Sir, I would let them settle down a little now before you go in.' 'Who on earth, Custos, was that?' I said. 'Don't you know Sir?' He said, 'that is Joanna Lumley.' I asked the Custos what she was doing there and he told me that her son was a new boy.

She had walked across the Speech Room stage with all eyes on her. The building is in the shape of the letter D with the stage being the straight part of the D, and the audience in semicircular rows ascending to the back row, which is well above eye-level when you are standing on the stage. I learnt later that Joanna Lumley had acted on this stage on several occasions and she knew every squeak in every board. Moreover, she had certainly drawn the attention of hundreds of parents to where she was sitting and, I fear, the new Head Master tended to follow suit. I walked onto the stage and a hush descended. I found that I was looking to my right, directly at Miss Lumley. Realising this was probably a mistake, I turned quickly to look hard to my left only to find that I was staring into the penetrating eyes of a man with his head on his hand and a mane of long flaxen hair. It was Michael Heseltine whose boy was also beginning his Harrow career with me. I also knew that somewhere in the Speech Room was my Chairman of Finance, later to become the Chairman of the Governors, Robin Butler (now Lord Butler), who son was also new with me, together with a few pairs of other parents known to us. All these thoughts rushed through my mind as I stood there and gazed at them all. I was very nervous. I had hidden my notes in my hand and was determined not to use them unless forced to and once into the swing of my delivery all was well. I left the hall accompanied by Angela and we stood outside and shook hands with yet another group of parents. Another adventure had begun.

The next day I had to address all the boys in Speech Room, which was just as alarming an experience. I recall apologising to them all for inadvertently referring to 'their' rather than 'our' School Songs, but also told them that the one thing I could not stand were 'public school boys'. I could have heard a pin drop. I then explained that boys who felt that just being at Harrow gave them an edge over their contemporaries had better think again. All depended on their attitude to work, to creativity and to sport and those who tried really hard would benefit from all that Harrow had to offer. But those who expected the name of Harrow to be a passport to university, a good job and promotion would be sadly disillusioned. Arrogance was not to be part of the modern Harrow while I was Head Master and I fought it on several occasions in my early years. I spoke to them without notes on a variety of themes in the Speech Room. I realised, however, that I had to be very careful when I overheard a senior say to a very respected colleague as he left Speech Room 'What on earth will that man say next!'

I had a study on the ground floor of No 1 The High Street in the middle of a boarding house for ninety boys run by Edward Gould who later became the Master of Marlborough College. There were a great many bookshelves crammed with my books, there were some chairs but there was no desk. On asking the Bursar I found that the Head Master was expected to supply his own. The higher you climb in the educational world, the less is provided. I told the Bursar that I thought he ought to find me one and left it at that.

On the first day of term I was sitting in my study, without a desk, when there was a loud knock on my door. I shouted, 'Come in' and in came two large gentleman in uniform from Harrods. 'Excuse me Sir', one of them said, 'but is this the headmaster's?' 'Yes', I said. 'Good,' he said, 'we have come to deliver a desk.' I was delighted that action had been taken so quickly, and waited for the two gentlemen to return. Before they did, however, there was another knock on the door and in came Timothy Proctor, a small thirteen-year-old boy who was new that term. 'Excuse me, sir,' he said, 'but have you seen two delivery men from Harrods with a desk?' My heart sank. I said, 'Well, yes I have and they are about to return to my study with it.' 'Good,' said Tim, 'I will intercept them and have them take it up to my study.'

I was a little crestfallen, but shortly after there was another banging on my door and the two delivery men, with Tim, entered my study. They all looked pretty angry. The boy said 'Sir, my mother paid for a desk to be delivered' and, before he could complete his sentence, one of the men said 'but not assembled!' 'Yes, my mother paid for it to be assembled' replied a very cross and persuasive Tim. A rather acrimonious conversation then took place with the Head Master as the innocent bystander. My only contribution was a rather feeble 'Please! . . .' Finally, one of the men said in a resigned voice 'Oh well, Bert, we best assemble.' And the three of them left my study to assemble Tim's desk. I still had no desk.

So this is what it is like, I thought, to be the Head Master of Harrow.

Very early on in that first winter term, Neil Kinnock, at that time leader of the Labour party, challenged me to a public debate in Hillingdon. I have never been a party politician and have always resented the assumption that because I was a headmaster of three independent schools I must be a Conservative. The Blair Government is the first, in the whole of my experience, which seems by word and deed to want to be in partnership with the independent sector for the betterment of all children in the country. It will be interesting in the years to come to see where this refreshingly new approach leads both the independent and maintained sectors. However, the thought of taking on in public debate one of the senior politicians of his day, totally antagonistic to the independent sector, concerned me. I was worried lest my new colleagues would see me make a fool of myself. I discussed the idea with one or two senior masters who encouraged me to accept. 'After all,' they

said, 'if you refuse it will look as if Harrow and you are frightened.' So off I
went. The hall was packed, with standing room only. I enjoyed the experience, in retrospect at any rate, but it is for others to decide how I fared.

During those early weeks I had also to become acquainted with yet
another secretary. I was George Duvall's fifth Head Master of Harrow. His
career spanned forty years of service to the school. His style was very different from my secretaries at Ellesmere and Lancing. For most of my time at
Ellesmere, I was looked after by Mrs Jones, who was the embodiment of
efficiency and kindness and never told me off, not even for throwing away
too much paper which should have been filed!

At Lancing I had inherited a highly intelligent widow whose sons were in
the school. She knew everything that was going on, even to the point of
telling me the decisions I should take almost before I knew I had to take
them. She too could not have been kinder and, sadly, has recently died. She
would decide when it was time to dictate letters, bring in her typewriter,
place paper in the machine and type directly as I dictated. As she typed she
would, out loud, correct my English and, if she thought it necessary, tell me
what I should say in the letter. A truly amazing lady of whom I grew very
fond. Not as fond as I was to become of Ruth Holliss, however. She was holding down a big job in a high street bank, but grew progressively hostile to the
climate in banking which distanced her from her clients. She joined me at
Lancing and was brilliant. We worked very well together and she was happy
to take the tapes I had dictated early in the morning before she arrived. This
gave me much more time during the day to see people and to teach. Ruth
made time in the day to talk with teachers and pupils; they and she grew very
fond of each other and the atmosphere in the office was fun. On the day of
one scholarship examination a headmaster of a preparatory school brought
his candidate together with a bottle of Chanel No. 5 for Ruth. 'Um,' she said,
'that stinks!'

George Duvall at Harrow was also happy to use my early morning tapes
and so arrange his day according to his own workload. He knew Harrow
inside out and prevented me from making a large number of mistakes. I must
have taken some getting used to. During that first term I decided to coach
rugby most afternoons of the week. I knew it would be my only opportunity,
as experience had taught me that once some of my new ideas were under
way in the School, my time could not be spent on the games field. In those
early weeks, however, it was a great way of getting to know the boys and
many of my colleagues who were also out on the fields.

One Saturday afternoon I was walking back from the fields with some
senior boys when we heard someone crying from within a laurel bush. I sent

the seniors on and dived into the bush to find a very small new boy who was clearly distressed. I took him up to our house, which had a balcony overlooking London. I asked him where he came from and discovered that he was from the Highlands of Scotland. I asked him what the buildings in the distance were, but he did not know. I gave him a pair of binoculars and he eventually spotted the GPO tower. 'Gosh, Sir! Is that London?' I talked with him and found that he had not visited Harrow before he arrived at the school. He had been driven there by his parents and left in his boarding house a few weeks previously. What an upheaval for him! He really had no idea where he was. There and then I decided to arrange a special programme for all future new boys so that they would get some sense of where they were, be taken to visit places and so generally helped to settle in. My young crying boy cheered up and very quickly settled down to do well in the school.

In the afternoon, I would change into a tracksuit and go down to the fields, running up over the Hill to visit the rackets and squash courts on the other side, calling in on George to sign the letters before he went home. Standing there in his office, with perspiration dripping off the end of my nose onto his blotter, I can still hear him muttering, 'I suppose I shall get used to this kind of thing!' He did, but eventually had to retire through age and we had the difficult task of finding his successor. Mrs Pat Hobbs was appointed; her husband worked locally for Glaxo. She was a lady of abundant energy, efficiency, readiness to admit a mistake, great understanding of the mistakes I made and a wonderful coffee maker. She complemented George Duvall perfectly and I realised what a lucky man I was. When she also eventually retired, Mrs Margo McKay took her place and I began to think that I had been born under a lucky star for she too was superb. I was really cared for, and any Head will confirm that a secretary who has the ability not to flap and to care for his or her welfare, while never turning a pupil or colleague away, is worth their weight in gold. I owe all these people a huge debt of gratitude.

Meanwhile I had to create a daily routine for myself at Harrow. I asked the housemasters where I had lunch. There was a silence and I was told that I went home. I was flabbergasted as my predecessor, Michael Hoban, had expended a huge amount of energy, time, patience and strength moving Harrow from house feeding to central feeding. He had been responsible for creating the Shepherd Churchill Dining Hall. This was a superb building in which the whole school could be fed in one sitting. Moreover he had established a dining room for the Head Master to entertain guests in and for use by the masters. The masters ate lunch there whilst the boys, together with the adult house staff, ate in the main hall. Time and again I thanked my lucky stars that I had not had to change the Harrow tradition and build the central dining hall; it was the best present any Head could have handed to his successor and I was grateful to Michael.

Being told to go home for lunch left me feeling that I was not wanted. At the meeting I stared hard at the youngest housemaster, Sir Alan Outram, who had been my captain of rugby at Marlborough when I was teaching there. 'Alan,' I said, 'I am sure that you would like Angela and I to have lunch with you tomorrow.' Poor man, he could only say yes. The ice had been broken and I worked round the table booking us in for lunch with every House. 'What happens, Head Master, when you have been round once?' asked a senior man. 'Ah!' I said, 'that will be a surprise, but I shall not bother you again.' At the time, I had about as much idea what I meant as they did; I went home and discussed it with Angela.

It so happened that the Hall had been designed around a central well which was occasionally used as a dance floor. I asked the Bursar to buy a dining room table, six chairs, two carvers and a large carpet of plain Harrow blue. At 11.00 a.m. on the morning when we had finally 'run out' of Houses with which to eat, we laid all this out in the centre of the dance floor. I bribed six senior boys to come and have lunch with us and we braved the stares and buzz of conversation as the whole school saw what the new Head and his wife were up to. I appointed one monitor as our luncheon secretary and from then on we had lunch with six different boys every day. We restricted the invitations to the two sixth form years, which meant that each boy had lunch with us several times before he left the school. In this way we got to know every boy who was at Harrow during our time and lunch was our great relaxation of the day.

I learnt two things about education during those lunches. I used to ask boys who had inspired them at Harrow, which teacher really had 'switched them on'. One boy would say Mr X and another would choke over his potatoes as he had not considered that Mr X could inspire anyone. Rarely did the same name come up twice; six boys inspired by six different teachers. It was encouraging to hear. I also used to ask each boy to name something at which he was better than anyone else round the table, including the Head Master and his wife. To begin with boys would say 'Nothing, Sir', but if we delved, rarely did we find anyone who did not excel at something. It was a very encouraging exercise, especially for some of the quieter, more average boys who invariably found something which they could do better than the Head Master and Mrs Beer.

One thing that most could do better than I could was to milk a cow. When I arrived, the school had a herd of about eighty milking cows and the milk was collected by tanker each morning. At that time very few boys were involved with the farm but I learnt from the Bursar, Sidney Patterson, that 'in the good old days' the boys used to go down to the farm on a rota and milk the cows each morning. Sidney was a marvellous gentleman of the old school; he had taught at Harrow virtually all his life, become a bachelor housemaster of The Grove and had been appointed Bursar by the time I arrived. Sadly, he retired at the end of my first year and died on Harrow Hill very soon after. He was the greatest help to me and became a close personal friend. We consumed a lot of sherry together and he encouraged me to reintroduce compulsory milking for all the new boys in their first year. We installed a pasteurising unit and the milk was taken to the dining hall for consumption at breakfast. For some of the city boys it was an education in itself and we were proud to be in charge of the nearest milking herd to Piccadilly Circus!

20

The Christmas Dinner and Speech Day

WE finished my first term with Christmas dinner for the whole school in the magnificent Shepherd Churchill Dining Hall. The adults were in black tie and the boys in tails. I was quite looking forward to the occasion, but the words of a famous headmaster, Walter Hamilton of Rugby, kept coming to me 'Ian, whatever you do, try and avoid congregating the whole school together in one place at any one time. It is tempting disaster!'

Angela and I had some colleagues and parents to drinks in our house and then walked over to the Shepherd Churchill. As we got closer I realised the boys had 'won' on this occasion. There is a grand flight of steps down to the entrance to the Hall and near the top of the steps is a waterfall connecting two large ponds. Some thoughtful boys had put bubble bath in the water and this had been wonderfully effective. It was clearly high-grade bubble bath. All the guests to the Christmas dinner in 1981 had to walk through a wall of bubbles about ten feet high. It was a good joke and did no harm but I realised I would have to keep my wits about me at future such functions.

The occasion of my first Speech Day grew nearer and I began to worry about any tradition, comparable to that at Lancing, of boys creating problems for me. The housemasters told me not to worry, and I knew that they were sufficiently proud of their boys to try and make certain that nothing happened. I relaxed until the night before the great event.

Speech Day at Harrow involved all the parents arriving in their finery, making certain that they were present by the time Bill, or roll call, took place. Many centuries previously, when the school consisted only of the Old Schools with the play yard in front, boys had a roll call two or three times a day to check that they were all still present and correct. This was done by a master standing on the steps of the Old School, calling out each name individually from the school list, or Bill Book as it was called, and the boy walking forward, raising his Harrow hat and calling out 'Here, Sir!' As the school grew larger these roll calls took place in the boarding houses, but the tradition of the Head Master holding Bill in front of the Old Schools with the entire school assembled in what is called Bill Yard still continues today. When I was Head Master I took Bill on a Friday afternoon in the weeks up until Speech Day. This was done so that all the boys knew how to behave and, in my case, so that the Head Master knew how to behave as well. Bill takes place at 11 a.m. on Speech Day with all the parents outside Bill Yard with their cameras, but my wife only witnessed it on our last occasion as she was always preparing things elsewhere. The Head Master calls out the names of 800 plus boys and then, almost immediately, goes to Speech Room to address the parents on the state of the school. The Head Master and his wife then entertain guests to drinks and lunch, whilst the parents have lunch elsewhere and activities, of course, take place throughout the day before Harrow Songs are sung in the Speech Room and everybody goes home at about 6 p.m. The school was very much 'on show'.

I went to bed the night before, having written my speech, and knowing how to take Bill efficiently. I just hoped that the school would be looking smart. At about three in the morning I awoke worrying that something might be happening. I told Angela that I would take a short run around the hill to check that all was well. She thought me mad and told me to stay in bed and get some energy for the morrow. I knew, however, that I would not sleep and so I put on some running shoes and my tracksuit and set off around the hill.

All seemed well and peaceful until I arrived in one of the huge gardens behind a particular boarding house. On the lawn below the house, where the parents would be having a tea party later that day, I found a message in whitewash in the grass. It was not very complimentary to a member of my staff and the letters were about four feet high. I groaned inwardly and ran back to my house, which had by that time been completed, and brought back a hand lawnmower. The dew on the grass caused the lawn mower to slip and it would not work properly. Shouldering arms with it once again, I ran back to the garage and substituted the lawnmower with hand shears and a rake. I then spent a not so happy hour or more cutting the grass for this particular housemaster, raking up the cuttings and hiding them all under a bush. I ran back to my garage and deposited the tools before setting off again around the hill. By this time it was about 4.30 a.m.

Everything was fine until I reached, just before I got home, the Old Schools and Bill Yard. I could hardly believe my eyes. Bill Yard itself is surrounded by iron railings, and a boy, or boys, had succeeded in weaving reams of thin cardboard in and out of the railings so that it was quite impossible to see into Bill Yard itself from the outside. It was obvious that parents who came to witness Bill would see nothing.

All I could do was to set to work with a will. I began by unweaving the cardboard; each roll was just over three feet high and there were two layers vertically one above the other forming a six foot continuous strip. As I unwound the cardboard I began to create a very large amount of refuse. Fortunately, there was a skip on the main road which was being used for renovations in one of the Houses. I folded the cardboard into huge piles and ran down with them to deposit them in the skip. That was the least of my concerns for there was a much bigger problem. While it had been comparatively easy to unwind cardboard by the gates of Bill Yard, as you move round the ground begins to fall very steeply for the railings are built on top of a very high brick wall with a garden below. The only way to unwind the cardboard was to hang by one hand from the top rail and slowly move along, rather as a monkey might. This took some doing and was slow work. There was nothing I could do about it and I was reluctant to have anyone come and help me as I wished this to be a secret known only to my wife and myself. I was fortunate. Curtains remained drawn; for once I was grateful that boys sleep late. I finished my task at about 7 a.m. and ran back to our house.

Accustomed to my nocturnal wanderings in the various schools I had attempted to control, my wife was not worried about my absence, but she was a little concerned that I was totally exhausted. However, there was nothing more to be done so I had a shower, had some breakfast, collected my mail and went up to my study to dictate my letters before my secretary arrived for work. Fortified by strong coffee I eventually walked up to Bill Yard at 11 a.m. to take my first Bill. Hundreds of parents were present and the entire school stood looking smart in their tails and Harrow hats. I sang out their names and each answered 'Here, Sir!' I could not help wondering which of these wonderful young men were the originators of the temporary 'closure' of Bill Yard. To this day I have no idea who they were and I suspect that until this day they had no idea who cleared it all up.

It was all well worth doing as I had very little trouble throu   ıt the whole of my ten years at Harrow, and the boys, as far as jokes of this type were concerned, behaved themselves pretty well. It was particularly appropriate that, when I left, the boys most generously subscribed to and had made for me a silver model of a Harrow boy in tails, raising his hat to the Head Master. The inscription below was the answer 'Here, Sir!'

21

Changes at Harrow

HAVING been told by one of the governors at interview that I could change anything at Harrow, provided it was not unimportant, the first decision I made was one of crucial importance so far as the curriculum was concerned. We doubled the number of science periods taught to all new boys in their first year in the school.

When I began my teaching career at Marlborough College science was not examined in the common entrance examination. I remember writing a paper trying to get science introduced as a compulsory subject in that examination in 1958. The pattern at that time was for a boy to arrive at his public school very far advanced in Latin, indeed not far below O-level standard. At the same time he was about one or two years behind his contemporaries in the maintained sector as far as science was concerned.

I suppose that I was very influenced by my own background. I had been evacuated at the start of the war to Abergele in North Wales. I was aged eight. The only school I could attend, as my parents were not well off and could not afford to send me to the preparatory school, was the county school. The other boys and girls all knew each other well and I had to struggle. The curriculum was amazing and beat today's National Curriculum into a cocked hat. How about this for a timetable between the ages of nine and eleven: English Language and Literature, History, Geography, Religious Studies, French, Welsh, Latin, Physics, Chemistry, Biology (taught as separate subjects), PE (or PT as it was then), Woodwork, Metalwork, Bookkeeping and Shorthand! No wonder I was suspicious of very advanced Latin in the independent schools in the absence of any science, let alone bookkeeping.

As the brightest pupils at top independent schools were put on a one-year or two-year course to O-level, these pupils almost inevitably did very well in classics and less well in science. This in turn meant that many who would otherwise have done so did not take sciences at A-level, depriving the sciences of some of the brightest young men. Admittedly, some of them transferred to science at university. I recall very well Richard Hughes, an extremely bright young man at Marlborough. He was a classicist who came to me for tuition to help him pass the pre-medical examination into a London hospital. He studied for three months in order to do this and is now one of the country's leading neurosurgeons.

When I arrived at Harrow, I found that there was an accelerated stream for the brightest new pupils who took O-levels after only two-years. They simply did not have a good enough foundation in the sciences. I was greatly helped at that time by one of the governors, whose boy was in the school, agreeing with me that these young men should not be accelerated but be given a proper grounding in science, taking three years to O-level along with everyone else. This also meant that the young men stayed in the school for five years, whereas the brightest pupils before the change had left after only four years, or four years and one term if they were doing the Oxbridge entrance examination. As a consequence, the brightest would frequently not be able to lead the school in the last two terms of the year.

We therefore abolished the accelerated stream and delayed the start of A-level study until the beginning of the fourth year in the school. I felt very much happier that the distribution of the brightest young men in the sixth form was across all academic disciplines.

The second major change we made concerned the way in which the senior pupils at Harrow had traditionally been acknowledged and applauded. There was a group of monitors who ran the boarding houses and looked after the general discipline and pastoral care of the younger boys. They wore a blue tie with silver lions on it, while all the other boys wore a black tie, supposedly in mourning for the death of Queen Victoria. There was another group of sporting boys who could be elected to the Philathletic Club and were allowed to wear a bow tie. When I asked how all the musicians, actors and artists were acknowledged, I was met with a blank stare. It seemed to me that the absence of such acknowledgement put an unhealthy emphasis on sporting prowess and somehow we had to redress the balance. The system was clearly a relic of the old days when being good at sport was the one way to succeed in a public school, and we all knew that times had changed.

The housemasters and I discussed this for many hours together and it became clear that I had only two options. One was to abolish the Philathletic Club and the other was to create a cultural organisation which would stand alongside that club. By now I knew enough Old Harrovians to realise that if I abolished the Philathletic Club I would probably bring down on my head a great deal of wrath and, being ex-sporting gentlemen, as I myself was, I could imagine that the wrath would be fairly vigorous.

The alternative was to create a group to be called 'The Guild' the number of members of which would match the number in the Philathletic Club. They would all be young men who had distinguished themselves in the creative sphere, outside the classroom but not involving sport. I designed a claret coloured tie with silver lions. This complemented the monitors' tie.

I recall well the first young men whom I invited to become members of the Guild. One sat in my study and, with tears in his eyes, he said, 'Are you telling me that this great school is going to acknowledge my ability?' He is now a concert pianist. Most of the members were, however, either a little disdainful, feeling it unnecessary, or just took it in their stride. A boy who had been particularly disdainful came to see me three weeks later to praise the decision I had taken. When I asked him why he had changed his mind, he said that he had never received so much abuse from other boys as he had received since being made a founder member of the Guild. He now realised how important it was that the cultural life of the school should be officially acknowledged to counterbalance the philistine element in the school. As the years went by hostility to the Guild gradually disappeared and it became accepted as part of Harrovian life.

Many hours were spent discussing how the younger boys should be acknowledged. After all, said some, younger boys were entitled to wear sporting ties because they had played for the school, so ought not the equivalent be possible for a prominent young musician, artist or actor. It was eventually agreed that ties were quite inappropriate. Instead the Guild created a Guild Plate, designed and made in the school pottery, which was awarded to prominent fifteen- and sixteen-year-olds who had distinguished themselves in artistically creative ways.

I genuinely believe that this decision was one of the most important we made at Harrow at that time and changed for ever the balance within the school between the sporting and creative elements of the community. At this time we also decided to commemorate the name of one of Harrow's greatest pupils, Anthony Ashley Cooper, who later became Lord Shaftesbury. Few people who sit on the steps which surround the statue of Eros in Piccadilly Circus know that the statue was given by the ordinary people of the country to commemorate Lord Shaftesbury after his death. He was the greatest social reformer of his day, and we felt that something at Harrow should continue year after year to stimulate the consciences of the present generation in the hope that they, too, might go out into the world to change it for the better.

The musicians and the dramatists staged a presentation in Chapel of the life of Anthony Ashley Cooper to coincide with the centenary of his death. It is always said that his life was changed when, whilst a junior pupil in the school, he witnessed the funeral of a pauper at St Mary's Church, Harrow, and determined at that moment to do something to better the lot of the poor. This event was re-created and the whole celebration took place in the presence of Her Majesty The Queen Mother. Every year since then there has been a Shaftesbury Lecture given by a visiting expert on a social problem of our day.

The third big change made early on was to establish far more lines of communication between the teachers and parents. Before my arrival the custom was for the parents to liaise directly with housemasters and this was efficiently and well done. In no way did I wish to harm this particular relationship, but I did wish to bring the assistant teachers closer to the parents of the boys they taught. In my previous schools I had been used to bringing parents in on regular occasions so that they could meet all the teachers. It was clear to me that this should also happen at Harrow.

There were only two slight problems. It was imperative for the assistant masters to be guided sufficiently clearly for there to be no difficult conflicts between the housemasters and the subject teachers. For a professional group of men and women, however, this was not a difficult problem to solve. The second problem was more delicate. One of the reasons for Harrow's great success as a boarding school is the fact that it still takes boys from all over the world. They came not only from Europe and further afield, but also in large numbers from Ireland, Scotland and the northern parts of England and Wales. We did not wish to create a system which put parents who had gone to the expense of sending their children to boarding school under an obligation to spend a great deal more money coming to meet the teachers on too many occasions. We therefore published dates for these functions well in advance, and made certain that a parent would only have to visit once in the year. It was an immediate success with parents, teachers and the pupils themselves.

It was important to plan for the next ten years and I wanted to make certain that the programme presented to the Governing Body was a programme which had been created by my colleagues in the Masters' Room who, after all, did all the work. I designed a simple questionnaire on one side of a piece of paper and asked each of my colleagues to complete it during my first three weeks in the school. This they did, and I spent my first half term analysing all eighty-four sheets of paper. It was before the days of easy access computers so I entered up all their ideas on paper and created a ten-year plan. I was able to distribute this to my colleagues after half term and we had very quickly created an agreed development plan to present to the governors. The Governing Body, whose function so far as I was concerned was to consider the advice of the professionals working in the school and then to try and find the wherewithal to implement their advice, was quite superb. They succeeded in finding the wherewithal for a ten-year plan to be completed in five. As Harrow is not a school with great endowments, however, fulfilment of the plan would require a lot of fundraising and this was an area in which I already had some experience from my years at Ellesmere and Lancing where there had been similar funding problems.

22

Fundraising

AFTER the war all independent schools had a major problem catching up on the maintenance of their existing buildings and creating new buildings appropriate to the modern curriculum. The problem was particularly acute as far as the sciences were concerned. As a result, an Industrial Fund was set up by the then Chairman of Guinness, Sir Hugh Beaver, and the Fund gave money to individual schools to help them build new science laboratories. This fund fairly soon dried up and the schools were left to their own devices to raise money.

Guinness, under Sir Hugh Beaver, took a great interest in education and offered, amongst other things, a scholarship for a schoolmaster to work at Guinness and learn something about an industry. I was fortunate enough to be awarded such a scholarship and worked as a temporary research brewer during the school holidays when I was teaching at Marlborough. I worked at Park Royal, investigating the flocculation of yeast cells in the brew, and at St James's Gate, Dublin, on varieties of barley. I earned more per week there than I did from teaching and learnt a great deal about business. They were gracious days. The laboratory shut down completely during the Dublin Horse week, and when I turned up for the first time I found a cheque, payment of salary in advance, and invitations to three Hunt Club Balls. I imagine times have now changed. Fortified by the Guinness experience, I was encouraged to go and work for the Coal Board and United Steel in other years. All this was work experience of great value to me later on in my career.

During this period several American firms moved into the United Kingdom bringing with them ideas on how to raise money for private institutions. They turned their attention to the independent schools, encouraging them to use their ex-pupils and parents to give money as was already the established pattern in the United States. It was not so easy in the United Kingdom as our tax laws did not benefit the giver to the same extent as the laws in America. However, many schools employed such firms to help them to raise capital funds. Ellesmere College was one of these and I was soon heavily involved with a fundraising manager to raise money for the school.

I was convinced that the average independent school prospectus was way behind modern marketing methods, even in 1961. The Ellesmere prospectus would have attracted very few parents, as it had not really been updated since before the war. I therefore suggested to the fundraising firm we were using that they should design a new prospectus for Ellesmere College which they could use to persuade other schools to follow suit, provided that they covered all the costs themselves, using it as their own marketing tool. This they were prepared to do and we got a new prospectus free of charge.

Fundraising then, as now, really depends entirely on the personality of the head and, if possible, a very long-serving teacher within the school whom generations of pupils have revered. At Ellesmere we were particularly fortunate as Jim Nankivell, or 'Nankie' as he was known to everyone, had been a boy at the school, a master there after his degree at Oxford and was a senior member of staff when I arrived. He became a great personal friend and tremendous support for me. We would travel the countryside going to dinner after dinner, speaking to parents and old boys in order to persuade them that the modern Ellesmere College was worth supporting financially. The appeal was a great success but took its toll on myself and Nankie.

After one dinner held in the mountains between mid-Wales and the north, we had to drive home at about midnight. It was a bitterly cold January evening and neither of us were looking forward to the journey home. In those days I tended to drive rather fast, and was the proud owner of one of the earliest Volvo motor cars to be driven in England. Travelling down a long straight road I had not anticipated a sharp bend to the left just before the road crossed a deep ravine. The car would not take the bend at the speed I was travelling and we went almost clean through a thick hedge. When we had extricated ourselves from the car by climbing over the front seats and escaping through the back door, we realised that forty nine percent of the car was hanging over the ravine.

These were the days before mobile telephones, and so we had to walk some distance to find a telephone and contact my wife who raised the local garage in Ellesmere and asked them to come and save us. She was, at that time, nursing a six-week-old baby so was still 'up' after the ten o'clock feed. About an hour later the local breakdown lorry arrived with a substantial crane on the back. It soon became apparent that we could not lift the car out of the hedge, as one of the front wheels was trapped. The mechanic crawled through the hedge, removed the front wheel and the car was then lifted back onto the road collapsing onto the front axle. The wheel was replaced and it was suggested that I could then drive home provided I did so very carefully. I learned then to respect the strength of the 1963 Volvo.

But what I had not considered was the age of Nankie. He had turned from fairly normal pink, through various stages of whiteness, until he was now blotched with purple. I cannot recall seeing any man quite so cold and, as he was small and wiry, with very little spare flesh on him, he was completely numb. During the rescue he sat in the front cabin of the recovery vehicle in an attempt to warm up. He then transferred himself to the passenger seat of the Volvo and I drove him home. We reached his house in Ellesmere between three and four in the morning. He had uttered not one word until, on getting out of the car, he leant back in and said simply 'Thank you, Headmaster, for the most bloody awful evening of my life!'

One of the most important things for a new headmaster to spend time on is getting to know the old boys of the school, and to do so without implying that the boys now coming into their school are a vast improvement on their predecessors! One of my abiding memories will be the support and friendship I received from Old Ellesmerians, Old Lancing Pupils and Old Harrovians. It seems odd to be a Vice-President of all three Old Boys Associations when I am not one of my old school, but I am very proud to be so recognised. These old boys took me out of their school and entertained me on neutral ground. They were very frank about the good and the bad of their time at school, as well as the good and the bad of my headmastering as they perceived it. They were an integral part of my career as headmaster and I cannot recall a single unhappy moment. I am greatly in their debt.

At Lancing, fundraising followed a similar pattern and, once again, we had to travel around the countryside getting to know pupils and trying to persuade them to have confidence in the new management of the College. It was not, however, quite as easy as it had been at Ellesmere as we also had to raise money for the completion of the Chapel. This was an entirely separate exercise from raising money to build new laboratories and classrooms. The Chapel was started in 1868. By the time he died in 1891, the Founder Nathaniel Woodard had built the east end to its present height but the west end, apart from its foundations, did not exist. The end of the building was sealed by the biggest sheet of corrugated iron known to exist in Europe. The foundations went down 225 feet whilst the building above ground was to rise to 170 feet. The scale of the enterprise becomes understandable when it is realised that the nave is the fourth highest of any church or cathedral in the United Kingdom. The building is modelled on fourteenth century English Gothic, with thirteenth century French influences. The Gothic French cathedrals took several hundred years to build. Lancing was attempting to do it in just over a hundred.

We were constantly running out of money and halting progress, but such was the generosity of so many different individuals and trusts that we never had to stop building for very long. We could, however, never use College money and everything had to be raised from outside sources. In 1974 the stonework for the great rose window was laid out on the lawn below the chapel. It could not be lifted into place by the stonemasons, as we had no money to build the two spires and the buttresses which were to support it on the north and south sides. The cost of these buttresses was colossal and I could not see how we were going to achieve our object. It was a question of having to find all the money at once; we could not build it stone by stone. We came to a halt.

About that time a particular magazine, distributed fairly widely to our embassies and the English-speaking Union, published a centre spread on the Chapel with some fine photographs. The magazine was seen by a Mr and Mrs Jarvis in the USA. They had never visited the United Kingdom but were planning, in their retirement, a holiday in our country. They had become very interested in the Chapel and wrote me a letter asking if they could come and see it. There was nothing unusual in this as the Chapel is open to the public every day of the year. I told them that they would be welcome and that they could have a tour with the Verger. I thought no more about it until early one afternoon my secretary telephoned me to say that Mr and Mrs Jarvis from America were outside and wished to see me. I then remembered the letter, asked them in and told them a little about the Chapel. I bid them farewell and went on with my work.

About two hours later they asked to see me again. I was, I recall, exceptionally busy and was groaning inwardly at the prospect of wasting more time on a second conversation, but I could not see how to avoid it without appearing rude. In they came, clearly excited by their visit and making complimentary comments about the building. Mr Jarvis, however, seemed rather ill at ease. Eventually he said 'Headmaster, this may be quite impossible, but I would very much like to be able to buy one of the spires and flying buttresses to commemorate my marriage to my wife. The only condition that I would wish to impose would be that her initials should appear on the spire and that we could have a photograph of you with her in front of the chapel'. I was totally dumbfounded and immediately expressed my concern that he might not be aware of the vast sum of money that was required to purchase this extraordinary piece of ecclesiastical stonework. He assured me that he had discussed the financial aspects with the Verger and there was no problem at all. I forgot my work and ordered tea and a bottle of wine and we sat down to celebrate. I was just a little concerned about the carving of the initials because we had stood out against such memorials in the past, but I somehow felt that the authorities would overcome their scruples this time, the more especially as the initials would be very high up in the sky.

During our small tea party Mrs Jarvis suddenly exclaimed 'Oh, gee! Wouldn't it be wonderful if I could buy the other spire and flying buttress to commemorate my husband. Do you think I could do that Headmaster?' I nearly choked over my tea and just looked at her. I said, 'Do you really mean that, Mrs Jarvis?' 'Indeed, I do,' she said.

So, on that day Lancing was given the only His and Hers spires that I know of in any church or cathedral in the world. I felt like writing to Harrods and asking whether they could appear in their Christmas catalogue! The initials—J. J. for him and M. E. J. for her—are there to this day and can be seen from the ground but, to my knowledge, Mr and Mrs Jarvis have never returned to see the Chapel. Thanks, however, to their stupendous generosity we were able to finish the whole of the west end.

The great rose window, the largest in the United Kingdom, was built by a small team of stonemasons. The pieces of stone were laid out on the grass, each carefully numbered, and one by one were hauled up to their allotted place. One of the difficulties was that no one living had ever built such a window and no one really knew how it was done. The masons placed a piece of wood in the centre of the 32 foot circle and drove a six inch nail into the middle of this. A piece of string as long as the diameter of the window was then attached and the masons worked on that string-line. The BBC brought the 'Blue Peter' programme down when we were almost complete to record this piece of history. I climbed the scaffold with John Noakes, the Blue Peter presenter, to place the phosphor-bronze cross in the centre of the window. It was about a millimetre out of position. It was an amazing feat of building, which was followed by the glaziers with all the stained glass.

The window was consecrated in a celebration of the Eucharist in May 1978 in the presence of HRH Prince Charles with a sermon given by the Archbishop of Canterbury. Over three thousand people made their Communion that day. It was a wonderful celebration of thanks for the extraordinary fundraising and building endeavour which had enabled the Chapel to be completed. So many people had worked so hard, many before I had arrived at Lancing, but all were convinced that, with God's help, the task would be finished. I was so fortunate to be the Head Master in office when the great service of dedication took place.

On the same occasion Prince Charles opened the School's first boarding house for sixth form girls. The school had been monastic since its foundation the previous century. I recall Prince Charles asking me 'And what am I to call the House?' 'Manor House, Sir,' I replied and quick as a flash he came back with 'What a marvellous name for the first girls' House in a boys' school; spelt Manna, I presume?'

Sir William Gladstone had left me with a healthy entrance list for which I was most grateful, but we still had to advertise the school as much as we could, provided it could be done discreetly. We asked the boys to send formal invitations to their former prep school headmasters and their ladies to come to a champagne party with the Head Master and his wife at Lancing. Before the party their old pupils would show them around their new school. The idea worked wonderfully well for it was the first time that most of the heads had ever been able to bring their wives to such an occasion. They all came. It seems so obvious today but at that time it was a real breakthrough and did a great deal for Lancing's recruitment.

I felt that one of the first things I had to do on arriving at Harrow was to create a new image of the school. There was a tendency for preparatory school heads to believe that Harrow, being in London, was nowhere near the countryside. I wanted to convey something of the beauty of Harrow Hill and the countryside which insulated the school buildings from the concrete jungle of North Harrow. I decided that the best way to do this was not to write a new prospectus, although that was also eventually done, but to make a video. The date was September 1981 and a video of a school was a comparatively new idea. We managed to persuade a producer to make a video for us on the understanding that he could use it as publicity material for himself and enter it into any national competition he wished. I believe it was shown at a competition in the South of France. We had to act very quickly as we only had the cameras for two days. The first day we went up in a helicopter and travelled from the centre of London down to Harrow Hill taking aerial pictures; on the second day filming took place within the school. There was no time to write a complex script so the producer decided to interview me on the chapel terraces, explaining what I thought the school was all about. The finished product seemed to please most of my colleagues and we sent complimentary copies to almost every preparatory school in the country. It certainly had the effect we wanted and increased the number of enquiries about the school dramatically. Many small boys watched the video in their prep schools and then said to their parents 'I want to go to Harrow.' I only hope we did not create too much extra work for busy headmasters.

When I arrived at Harrow many people told me that I would not have to spend time raising money. How mistaken they were. The school has very few endowments. The most valuable endowment it possesses, other than the Hill itself, is what was once farmland given by the Founder John Lyon, but is now part of St John's Wood. However, by Royal decree any income or profit from that land had to be used to maintain the track to Harrow Hill, now the Harrow Road. Recently, the trust deed has been changed so that the monies can be used for educational purposes in the boroughs through which the road travels, but none can be used for Harrow School itself. Therefore the Head Master was left to go fundraising once again.

It was probably the case that former pupils of Harrow tended to be wealthier than those of the other two schools in which I served as head. However, they still had to be persuaded that what we were doing for Harrow was sensible and that they could have confidence in the modern management of their old school. From the moment I arrived in 1981, I was determined to build a really modern technology centre which would enable the boys at Harrow to design and make things with their hands. The old workshop might have been modern once was now a disgrace in a school with Harrow's reputation. My dream was of a huge building which would be totally flexible with all internal walls moveable, equipped with the very latest computers, computer aided machinery, robotics and so on. One Old Harrovian shared my dream and was generous enough, having learned that the building would cost £1 million, to promise £500,000 if I could raise the other half. It was a challenge. It was also a tremendous stimulus.

We were very fortunate that the then Prime Minister, Margaret Thatcher, was a great supporter of Harrow and she told me that she was prepared, with Denis, to host a drinks party to help me raise money. We gave her the names and addresses of one hundred Old Harrovians, parents and friends of Harrow who we thought might be prepared to subscribe. We had a model of the new centre made by the architects and one evening my wife and I left the school to go to 10, Downing Street to speak at yet another fundraising function.

We had arranged for a small gift for Margaret and Denis as we clearly wanted to thank them for supporting us, but my wife was insistent that Margaret Thatcher should also have a 'real' present. What she meant by this was that she was going to take some pots of her home-made marmalade as she had watched the Prime Minister describing on television how she made marmalade. I think my wife felt that hers might be even better. We arrived at Downing Street and our coats were taken away into the cloakroom along with the plastic bag containing the pots of marmalade. At the last minute our courage failed us.

The function was a huge success. The Prime Minister made a few comments, and told me to excite everybody about the vision I had for this new building. I did just that, lots of questions were asked and later that evening, having said goodbye to everyone, we went to reclaim our coats and leave. No one else was about. Suddenly, a young man came down the staircase and I realised he had been a pupil of mine at Lancing. He was in one of the Services and was on duty looking after the Thatchers in the flat upstairs. We asked him if he could place the marmalade on the breakfast table the following morning and he promised that that this would be done.

The evening had two consequences. The first was that when we met the Prime Minister at another function two months later she was ecstatic about Angela's marmalade. The second was that we raised just over £500,000.

If you visit Harrow today you should go and look at the Churchill Schools—Harrow's information, communication and technology department. To coincide with this development we also created with City and Guilds a new Certificate for Computer Competence which I had hoped would be achieved by every pupil in the sixth form before they left Harrow. We did not achieve this aim, but we did succeed in stimulating a large number of other schools, especially in the maintained sector, to enter for the award. At the first award ceremony, presided over by the minister at the Department of Trade and Industry, Geoffrey Pattie (now Sir Geoffrey), a housewife was one of the first to gain the certificate, closely followed by the Head Master of Harrow, and pupils from comprehensive schools as well as Harrovians.

My riskiest piece of fundraising was also at Harrow. We desperately needed some more hard tennis courts and, whilst the governors had approved the scheme in principle, we did not have the money. I promised them that I would raise the money, and, confident that I would be able to do so, asked the Bursar to begin work. By the time the courts were completed we were still £25,000 short. We had decided to inaugurate the courts by having a parents and boys tennis match. One of the parents had kindly offered one or two silver cups to be presented annually for such a competition. We had a very good turnout of parents, a splendid sunny afternoon and the time for prize-giving arrived.

I started by telling them that we were still £25,000 short and at the Governing Body meeting the following week I would have to explain why I had sanctioned the building of the courts before raising all the money. I was much concerned and said 'I suppose next term you may be looking at another Head Master'. There was a lot of laughter, but when the proceedings were over, a parent came up to me and said 'Head Master, we cannot lose you. I will give you £25,000!' I suppose that is another way of fundraising. I do not recommend it.

Angela was also deeply involved in fundraising but her activities were always connected with charity. At Harrow she chaired a group of the wives who worked extremely hard to put on functions together with my colleagues and the boys. I recall the Donkey Derby on the football fields which raised money for blind dogs, and the grand sale in the Shepherd Churchill hall for the Kidney Patients Association. Elizabeth Ward, the Founder of the Association, had had a boy at Harrow who died much later in his life of kidney failure. Special evenings were organised to celebrate each of the decades from the forties on and, on the last of these during our final year, we braved the boards to sing 'We said we wouldn't look back' from Julian Slade's *Salad Days*. A lot of fun was had by all and a great deal of money raised, as it also was by the Long Ducker event. The boys would run from Harrow Hill to Marble Arch and back, or carry out a comparable feat in the swimming pool, known traditionally as Ducker.

Another traditional event which Angela and I revived was the Silver Arrow. In the early days of the school, the most popular sport, indeed the only sport which was encouraged, was archery and the school would shoot to win the Silver Arrow. There are still some originals in existence in the school museum which are obviously very valuable. I fear the modern equivalent which we introduced was a very small replica costing but a few pounds. The old tradition had been discontinued in the eighteenth century due to rowdiness, as so many spectators came down from London to watch and they did not all behave especially well. Today's Silver Arrow is shot between Harrow School, the school of John Lyon and the local archery clubs. On the first occasion this was organised the Mayor and his lady dressed up suitably whilst Angela was persuaded to appear as Lady Bountiful. I am glad to say that the revived tradition of the Silver Arrow is still alive today and the school song 'Silver Arrow' once again means something to the modern pupil.

23

Harrow Songs

WHEN I was first appointed to Harrow I knew very little about the tradition of Harrow Songs. I was told that it would be wise if I learnt one or two of them and understood their importance in the life of the school, and this I did. As with many other activities outside the form room at Harrow, the introduction of music into the school was due to the initiative of the boys themselves. In 1857 they created the Harrow School Musical Society. The activities of that society were tolerated by the school but certainly not encouraged. In 1862 John Farmer was engaged as conductor. Farmer's personality and enthusiasm were so great that music became respected across the school. Farmer's chief method of bringing music into the school was House Singing. He composed a large number of songs for the boys to sing; tunes which the breaking adolescent voice could cope with without embarrassment. Different people wrote the words of the songs but the most influential was one of the assistant masters, E. E. Bowen.

I was first involved with Harrow Songs on my first Saturday evening at the school. On that Saturday every September next year's cricket eleven play the old Harrovians in a match known as the Goose Match, as a goose is always roasted for the dinner afterwards. When dinner had finished, instead of speeches, I found that the master in charge of cricket immediately introduced Songs. Someone took to the piano and the first song was announced. I was given my Harrow School Song Book. The 135-page book contains about 50 songs, although some are sung very much more frequently than others. The tradition is that anyone can 'be put on' by anyone else. This means that a member of the cricket team had only to stand up and request that the first verse would be sung by everyone over the age of fifty, say, and all of those who qualified would have to stand and sing that verse. This was clearly conducive to hilarity and I was a constant target. A small boy could leap to his feet and ask all who had played rugby football for England to sing the next verse and, usually, I was on my own, much to the boy's delight. (There were two others on the Harrow staff at that time who had played for England but their singing was marginally worse than mine.) On that

Saturday evening I looked around at the thirty or so people at the dinner and wondered how many extrovert sportsmen in the sixteen to eighteen age range would be prepared to sit round singing songs together and 'putting one another on' to sing solos. There was no embarrassment and a great deal of fun.

Later I learnt that, after dinner once or twice a term, each of the boarding houses would sit down together in the House and sing House Songs. In the first term of the year this was the baptism for all the new boys. Each of them knew that they had to sing a solo and the solo was always the same; the first verse of the *March of The Men of Harlech* which begins 'Hark! I hear the foe advancing'. Every time I hear that tune now I think of some small thirteen-year-old boy rising to his feet to sing in front of the sixty others in his house.

It was appropriate that the first House Songs that Angela and I could be invited to would be those held in the Head Master's house. This House was once run by the Head Master but now has a housemaster in charge. This is the biggest boarding house on Harrow Hill and contains ninety pupils. I was warned beforehand by Edward Gould, the housemaster, that I would be treated in exactly the same way as a new boy. I was due to join the Harrow community and would lead the way in singing my solo before the other new boys in the House followed me. The tradition is that the better you sing the politer the applause and, conversely, the more awful you are, the greater the cheer. Writing this down makes it all sound a curious, emotional and possibly intimidating introduction to a community, but there is no doubt in my mind that it worked. You became accepted. Harrow Songs were a kind of cement that kept the whole community together and the whole school used to meet once a term in the Speech Room to sing Songs. Women in those days were not really thought of as possible singers by the boys, so Angela was not asked to sing on her own for ten years, although she sang with other wives at Old Harrovian occasions.

The tradition of Harrow songs follows old Harrovians with them wherever they go in the world. Whenever or wherever a group of old pupils meet formally they will almost certainly sing Songs. I have sung them in Scotland, Wales, Ireland, Australia, Hong Kong, Jordan, the United States and South Africa.

When I arrived I was surprised to learn that the boys did not know the words of the main school Song, *Forty Years On,* adopted by many other schools across the world. I had been warned in advance of this situation by Major General Cosmo Nevill, who had been my Colonel when I served in Berlin in the 1st Battalion, The Royal Fusiliers. Although I did not know it at the time, he was an Old Harrovian and had followed my career after I left the army. When he read of my appointment as Head Master of his old school he wrote me a long letter giving me much helpful advice. I listened to my old Colonel as I had had, and still have, a very high regard for his judgement and views. He it was who gave me my Old Harrovian Association tie on my retirement and we can both wear the honour together, alongside our Royal Fusiliers Officers Club ties.

With this in mind, at the first Songs practice for the whole school I stopped them singing and told them that they all had to learn all the verses of *Forty Years On*, and that it would be sung in future without any Song Books open. This was very easy to check in the Speech Room, as the tiered semicircular seats gave me perfect vision of every pupil from the stage. I also told them that I was not very happy about their stance when they were singing the National Anthem. Too many of them looked as if they were protecting the Arsenal goal when a penalty was being taken. Curiously, I think these two comments about their behaviour brought the community together as much as anything else that I did. When next we rehearsed in Speech Room to practice Songs, not only did they stand well to attention for the National Anthem (even those for whom it was not their national anthem), but they sang *Forty Years On* with no Song Books open. Whenever I now return to Harrow I have to revise the words so that I am not seen to be reading from the book when the song is sung.

The Churchill story is now fairly well known. In the autumn of 1940 when Churchill was Prime Minister, his Secretary, Jock Colville, heard Winston singing Harrow Songs in his bath. His favourite song was *St Joles, the patron saint of the lazy boy*. The first verse goes as follows:

> When time was young and the school was new
> (King James had painted it bright and blue),
> in sport or study, in grief or joy,
> St Joles was the friend of the lazy boy.
> He helped when the lesson at noon was said,
> he helped when the Bishop was fast in bed;
> for the Bishop of course was master then,
> and bishops get up at the stroke of ten.
> St Joles hoo-ray. And St Joles hoo-roo,
> mark my word if it don't come true;
> in sport or study, in grief or joy,
> St Joles is the friend of the lazy boy.

Jock Colville told me that he said to Winston 'Why don't you let me ask the Head Master if he would summon the school to sing Songs to you in the Speech Room at the school. It would cheer you up.' And so it came about that in the dark autumn of 1940, the Prime Minister went back to his school, heard Harrow Songs and made a powerful speech to the boys. Those who were present that day say that the occasion made a deep impression on him and from that year onwards Churchill Songs have been sung at Harrow School every autumn. While he was still alive Churchill always attended. On his death Clementine, his widow, took his place. Today that place is taken by Lady Soames, Winston and Clementine's youngest daughter. An important guest is invited each year to join the school in Songs and to deliver a brief address to the school on a Churchillian theme. During my time as Head Master we received, among others, Her Majesty the Queen and Philip, Duke of Edinburgh, Their Majesties the King and Queen of Jordan, the Duke and Duchess of Kent, Jim Callaghan, Margaret Thatcher, Roy Jenkins and Michael Heseltine. The school would meet at 5 p.m. and sing Songs for about an hour. There followed a drinks reception and, finally, a small dinner party for the chief guest. I recall asking Queen Noor how many days King Hussein took as a holiday, and she replied that he took two days a year and that this was one of them. They were very happy occasions.

To celebrate the 50th anniversary of Churchill Songs we hired the Royal Albert Hall and placed the entire school and orchestra on the stage. The auditorium was packed with Old Harrovians, parents and friends of the school. Our guest of honour was Her Majesty the Queen Mother, but many other distinguished people were in the audience, amongst them, the Crown Prince of Jordan, Ted Heath and Denis Thatcher. Margaret Thatcher was also due to have been present but the date was Thursday, 22 November 1990. She was Prime Minister in the morning, but by the time we should have been receiving her at the Albert Hall, she was making her resignation speech in the House of Commons. It was truly amazing, and a reflection of the affection that the Thatchers had for Harrow, that Denis came, even if he was in something of a state of shock. When Songs finished, as they always do, with *Forty Years On*, *Auld Lang Syne* and the National Anthem, the Queen Mother left the Royal Box to huge applause. I was looking after her and the Crown Prince of Jordan whilst my wife stayed to look after Denis Thatcher. When he rose to leave tumultuous applause again broke out carrying with it great sympathy for him.

24

✦✧✦ ✦✧✦ ✦✧✦ ✦✧✦ ✦✧✦ ✦✧✦ ✦✧✦ ✦✧✦ ✦✧✦ ✦✧✦ ✦✧✦ ✦✧✦ ✦✧✦ ✦✧✦ ✦✧✦

Visitors

ONE of the privileges of being a headmaster is that you can write to anyone inviting them to come and speak to the school or to a group of pupils. Many people distinguished in their own fields enjoy meeting members of the next generation and in my experience very few of them tend to refuse. The only two who did refuse an invitation to speak at Churchill Songs were the US President and the German Chancellor. My wife—just—saved the President's reply from the incinerator. I did not really expect either of them to accept but it was worth a try.

On the other hand, many headmasters find the task of finding a distinguished visitor for prizegiving who will be inspired and inspire others difficult, as not everyone who is well known is good at speaking to the young. I was fortunate that both at Lancing and Harrow it was the tradition for the Head Master to award the academic prizes to the pupils. In those two schools, therefore, I was spared the task of finding somebody. At Ellesmere it was different, and so in my first year as Headmaster I had to find my first visitor. I was extremely fortunate that Christopher Chataway, whose decade of athletic fame overlapped with my decade of playing rugby, accepted my invitation. We had something else in common for we had also both worked for Guinness. He had married before I had and when he came to visit he and his wife brought their young children with them. They arrived earlier than we had anticipated and we had to make a few emergency arrangements. My wife was in the kitchen when their two children entered and the older one said, not realising to whom she was speaking, 'You know, Mummy said that they were not ready for us when we arrived!' Christopher Chataway spent most of the day talking with individual boys who clearly much enjoyed the privilege of meeting him. At that time he was also Member of Parliament for Chichester in West Sussex, but to the boys he was an Olympic athlete.

Field Marshal Montgomery of El Alamein came to visit us at Lancing. I had previously heard him at Marlborough when he had addressed the whole school and awarded them a half-holiday. The school was rapturous in its applause and he immediately leapt to his feet and awarded them a second half-holiday, much to the obvious annoyance of the Master. His visit to Lancing was early in my career at the time when hair was still very long. I well remember introducing a group of about six senior boys to him. He gazed at them, turned to me and said 'Headmaster their hair's too long!' I was pretty well fed up with the whole subject of hair by then and so I simply turned to one of the boys and said 'And how do you respond to the Field Marshal'? The boy looked at the Field Marshal, thought for one moment and then, to my horror, said 'Sir, it wouldn't be that you would just be jealous, would it?' There was a terrifying silence and then the Field Marshal roared with laughter and turning to me said, 'I think they are all right!'

Angela had as usual slaved over the stove for the previous twenty-four hours preparing a luncheon for our distinguished guest, who was known to have a delicate stomach, but when it came to the event all he wanted was soup. A tin of Heinz tomato soup was opened at the last moment and this was all he ate, but in his thank you letter he complimented my wife on her 'delicious lunch'! Over lunch I asked him what he thought of one of our prominent Cabinet Ministers of the day. He said very firmly 'I wouldn't go into the jungle with him'. So I tried him out with another well-known politician of the day only to receive the same answer. I tried a third third time and still the Field Marshal would not go into the jungle. Somewhat in desperation, I asked him with whom he would go into the jungle. Hardly a pause and answer came, 'Enoch!' He was, of course, referring to Enoch Powell, who several years later was our guest when he came to preach at Harrow.

Whilst at Lancing we also entertained Tom Driberg shortly after he had stopped being a Minister in Harold Wilson's Government. He was charming to meet and spoke very well to the pupils. He told me that when he and Evelyn Waugh were at Lancing they arranged the high altar cloth together as they were both sacristans. Driberg said it was not straight, but Waugh said 'If it's straight enough for me then it's straight enough for God.' I had no idea then of his homosexual orientation. It was not until the publication of his autobiography that I realised why he had so enjoyed the company of the young men that evening. In his book he describes his visit to Lancing, writing that the admirable young headmaster had no idea of who was staying in his house that night! In complete contrast was John Betjeman's visit when he was Poet Laureate; he was amazingly observant of his surroundings. We waited together for the London train at Shoreham-by-Sea railway station and he gave us an impromptu lecture about the Spanish influence on the architecture of the station (next time you are there look at the chimney pots . . .).

Occasionally I invited somebody to address the Common Room and one of our more memorable visitors was Dr Rhodes Boyson, then headmaster of a huge comprehensive school in London, before he became the Conservative Minister of Education. He astonished my colleagues by stating that, on one occasion, he had knocked a boy to the ground in his study because the boy was so ill-disciplined and violent. I asked him why he wore such ostentatious sideburns and he told me that he wanted people to remember him, as he intended to go into politics. He claimed that with such an absurd hairdo he would not be forgotten.

A much more gentle man was Cliff Richard, and I shall never forget the way he tuned his guitar to our piano in the drawing-room before playing it. His address to the pupils in the Chapel was powerful and sincere and delighted not only the Lancing pupils, but hundreds who came from neighbouring maintained schools. Nor will they forget the Sunday evening in Chapel when the West End cast of *Jesus Christ Superstar* performed at the special request of Tim Rice, who was an old boy of the school. Tim had asked the cast to perform in the Chapel at no cost in order to raise money for the completion of the rose window. They finished performing in London late Saturday night, packed up all the properties they required and drove to Lancing early on the Sunday morning. They spent all day preparing the Chapel for the performance at 8 p.m. After the performance, they dined with us before packing up again and returning in the early hours of Monday morning to the West End. It was one of the most generous gestures from a large group of people that I have experienced, but, as one leading actor said to me, 'For Tim we would do anything.' I have never before been able to thank them publicly.

Another wonderful act of generosity came from Lord Denning. He had accepted my invitation to come down to Lancing to address the Friends of the Chapel one Saturday in the autumn term. A week before the event, we were hit by a terrible attack of Hong Kong flu. It was the first of several outbreaks to take place in England and the media were therefore extremely interested. A large proportion of the Lancing College community was struck down and we had to introduce emergency measures. My wife was up in the dormitories acting as an extra sanatorium staff member, collecting and dishing out paper hankies, aspirin and water. Rarely did I succumb to school epidemics but, on this occasion, I, too, had been brought down with the flu. I was in bed with a very high temperature, still trying to deal with the media when, suddenly, the whole situation took a dramatic turn for the worse when one boy suffering from the flu contracted pneumonia and died. It happened so quickly and we were told, though this was small comfort, that there was nothing that we could have done to prevent it. The boy died on the Friday evening and I immediately cancelled Lord Denning's visit.

Unfortunately, it turned out that he was on holiday in France and could not be contacted. My wife invited the parents of the deceased boy to lunch when they came to visit on the Saturday, together with the Chaplain and the boy's housemaster. The salmon, caught by my brother-in-law in Scotland, which was to have been the celebration lunch for Lord Denning, became the lunch for the sad parents.

Just as lunch was about to begin, with me upstairs in bed with a temperature of over 103, my wife heard a knock on the door. Lord and Lady Denning were outside. Angela explained the situation and Lord Denning, without any hesitation, said, 'We are so sorry. Give our condolences and sympathies to the boy's parents, convey our sympathies and good wishes to the Head Master and tell him that on whatever date he wishes me to come to Lancing in the future I will come.' They quietly left the house and College.

I wrote shortly afterwards and invited him again on a date in the following year. His charming letter confirmed the date. He came and was brilliant.

We invited Norman St John Stevas to Harrow to judge one of our speaking competitions when he was Master of Pembroke College, Cambridge. He was delightful company and clearly very interested in the history of the school. I took him into the Fourth Form Room in the Old Schools. This was the original Fourth Form Room when the school was founded and is now part of the Harrow Museum and only used for tourists and other visitors. The pupils in those far off days used to carve their names in the wooden panels of the room. The names of Byron, Trollope, Churchill and others are to be found there. Today, the boys have their name carved for them on panels which hang in their boarding houses. However, in the bay window of the Fourth Form Room, on the left hand side, a small panel is missing. When I took St John Stevas in there we were talking about Cardinal Manning, who had been a pupil in the school. He told me that he had a small piece of wood with his name carved on it and when I showed him the empty space in the Fourth Form Room he said that he thought that it could well be the missing piece. He promised that he would try to remember to leave that piece of wood to Harrow School in his will. If it was the correct piece of wood neither of us could imagine how it had come into his possession. I hope he remembers.

Margaret Thatcher spoke at Songs when she was Prime Minister. As the local community knew that she was visiting the school, they organised a huge demonstration complaining to her about some decision or other that she had made. The demonstration took the form of a procession, not a quiet one, which was to confront her as she drove over the Hill. I was by Speech Room listening to the police on their radios as they succeeded in directing the procession away from the Prime Minister's car. This meant that the Prime Minister's car would arrive at Speech Room without her knowing anything about the demonstration at all. On her arrival, we took her first into the Memorial Hall on the way into Speech Room. Once in the Hall I said to her 'Prime Minister, you can relax now as Harrow is a friendly place and you can enjoy yourself.' I then received one of her famous ticking-offs as she exclaimed 'Head Master, in the Speech Room are over 800 boys waiting to hear me and they terrify me. How can I possibly relax? I am really worried!' I then realised how easy it is to become familiar with your own circumstances. Talking to 800 boys did not cause me very much trouble, but I would have been petrified in the House of Commons. Needless to say, she was quite brilliant and, when she spoke to them as a mother, had them in the palm of her hand.

A few years later she came to lunch and I was immediately struck by how much her own personal security had been increased. Not only the number of security men and women, but the armour-plated car, the searches and so on. However I voted in private I had always, as a headmaster, tried to ensure that my public face was one of independence, but on this occasion I could not help feeling sorry for her. She was isolated from the ordinary people. She came in a purely private capacity so there was no need for much police security but we were allowed to tell no-one of her visit, not even our daily help. Our younger son, who was by then at University, was woken in the morning to be told by his mother that she had a job for him. 'You mean,' he said, 'I have to move the compost heap yet again?' 'No, you can wait on the Prime Minister at lunchtime.' This he did with great aplomb and then joined her for coffee to tell her about some of the problems of the university he was attending.

The security for other visitors varied enormously. King Hussein brought his own bodyguards but they were rather conspicuous with their bulging jackets. Members of our own Royal family always seemed to be protected much more discreetly. However modern technology can make life very difficult for everyone. The day her Majesty the Queen came the boys were lining the streets of Harrow Hill, cheering her car as it passed them and raising their Harrow hats. Everyone looked polite, harmless and friendly. At the end of the day, totally exhausted, I collapsed in my house only to receive a telephone call from the *Sun* newspaper. They asked how the day had gone and I confirmed that it had been a memorable and above all a happy day. I felt the Queen had enjoyed herself. The reporter then asked me the first name of a pupil whose surname he quoted. I enquired why he wanted to know and he asked me what was my reaction, and the Queen's reaction, when she was welcomed on Harrow Hill by a pupil waving nude pictures of Bridget Bardot at her. I was dumbfounded. I asked what he was talking about and it transpired that one boy had pasted on the inside of his hat a picture of Bridget Bardot. The *Sun* photographer, having taken a vast number of photographs, apparently blew up the inside of every hat to see what he could find. I had nothing to say other than 'If this is the best way for you to spend money, and if this is the best way to fill space in your newspaper, then you do not deserve to be a national newspaper at all!' I slammed down the phone as I heard my wife staying 'Darling, I do hope that has not done a lot of harm.' It had not, as the *Sun* published, sensibly, nothing. I did however have an amusing interview with the young man concerned who was astonished that I knew what was inside his hat.

The last visitor I ever entertained made the request herself to come and visit the school on my last day as Head Master. I was hugely delighted to welcome Princess Margaret in July 1991. She was in quite excellent form, talking with all the boys and Masters and then joining in with Harrow Songs on my last afternoon. The police closed the streets so that her car could depart easily and the boys, as had become the custom for members of the Royal Family, threw the white carnations they were wearing all over her car as she departed. Unknown to me, the boys had persuaded the police to keep the roads closed for just a little longer. They then lined the pavements of the main road and made my wife and me run the gauntlet down the middle of the road as we walked from Speech Room to my study. It was a moving experience.

MARLBOROUGH COLLEGE

1955 – 1961

AND MISCELLANEOUS MATTERS

25

Preparatory Schools

An independent secondary school head looks upon preparatory schools as his or her lifeblood. These are the schools which, in the main, will supply the young pupils to keep the secondary school full. A good relationship between the secondary headmaster and all of his feeder schools is vital. Traditionally, the secondary school headmaster is expected to give prizes away in the preparatory school, to preach in the preparatory school chapel, give lectures, referee games and so on. As my three headships were respectively in Shropshire, West Sussex and north west London (the latter an internationally-known school which accepted pupils from preparatory schools across the entire country), I got to know the whole of the preparatory school world very well. Sadly, I have not kept a complete record but over 30 years I must have given prizes away or preached at well over 200 of them. The outstanding qualities they had in common were their friendliness and generosity as well as their determination to treat every child as a different individual who needed caring for and loving. They each, however, had their individual characteristics, although many differences are today being eroded through the pressures of the national curriculum, greater conformity required of teachers and teaching methods and a bureaucracy which is wearing down many schools in both the maintained and independent sectors. I very much hope that headmasters are still as idiosyncratic and wonderfully individual as I found them to be between 1960 and 1990, but it cannot be easy.

The preparatory schools have taught me many lessons, but none more salutory than one I learned in Birmingham while I was at Ellesmere. I was driving and my wife was acting as navigator. Neither of us had ever found getting around Birmingham very easy and, on this occasion, succeeded in finding our way most satisfactorily to Birmingham City football ground when we should have been at a large Odeon cinema some distance away. Eventually we found the cinema, the venue for the prizegiving. The school was a large day preparatory school and needed a big hall for the prizes. Both of us mounted the platform, where all the VIPs were sitting, just as the headmistress was completing her speech on the state of the school. I was next to perform and I have seldom seen a group of people so relieved to see me as the group on the platform that day. As I rose to my feet to say something I felt I had to apologise and explain why we were late. I suppose for a cheap laugh, I started 'We are sorry we are late but my wife was the navigator and she got it all wrong.' I learned afterwards that any boys who might have come to Ellesmere were probably now not coming as their mothers decided they did not wish their sons to be influenced by a male chauvinist who could be so rude and uncaring to his wife, especially in public.

Something similar happened when I went to preach at Repton Preparatory School. We were put off the scent on that occasion by making the mistake of asking a young Repton schoolboy the way to the junior school. He sent us on a wild goose chase halfway across Derbyshire and, when we eventually arrived outside the chapel, I heard a hymn being sung inside. I rapidly put on my gown and hood, grabbed my mortar-board in which were the notes for the sermon and walked in at the back. It was only then that I realised they were singing the hymn before the sermon. My wife sat down at the back and I walked up the nave, entered the pulpit, preached my sermon, came down out of the pulpit, walked down the nave again and out of the back door to collapse in a state of nervous tension in our car. The only other person who had similarly suffered was the poor headmaster who, during the verses of the hymn, had decided that he had to preach in place of his absent visitor.

Preparatory schools, understandably, like to have everything very well organised but some are more organised than others. I think of the school where there was a biscuit tin full to the brim of old threepenny bits. The whole school was lined up to go into chapel and each boy was given one coin. These hexagonal coins were then solemnly collected by the senior pupils at the end of the service and returned to the biscuit tin for use the following Sunday. Each boy had the money deducted from his pocket money and a cheque was sent to the charity concerned. They probably do it today, with the same threepenny pieces, but the rest is no doubt done through internet banking.

At another wonderful school the headmaster, who had been trained in the services, firmly believed in what he called Zero Hour. This was the hour when the platform party, including the visitor, would enter the hall for speeches. There were minus hours or minutes before Zero Hour, and plus minutes after Zero Hour. For example, the matron inspected behind the ears (I do not joke) at Zero Hour minus one hour, and she inspected again, in a general way, at Zero Hour minus 15 minutes. I wondered whether I was to be inspected as well as I stood in line and waited for the headmaster to count down the seconds on his watch. At Zero Hour precisely the procession walked into the hall. Everything, as far as I could tell, had gone like clockwork (literally) until the headmaster rose to give his speech which overran by 14 minutes and threw all the Zero Hour plus numbers into chaos. I must confess that I loved every minute of it and got up happy in the knowledge that the length of my speech was now irrelevant.

Speech days were only in my experience upstaged by sports days. On sports days anything can happen. One school I went to insisted on having an egg and spoon race for the staff which was, of course, extremely popular with the children. As the guest of honour I was seated on a grassy bank above the running track with the headmaster, his parents and some governors. We were cordoned off by little white posts and rope whilst the flagpole with the national flag was situated behind my back. I watched everyone line up for the egg and spoon race and could not help noticing an extremely attractive young lady balancing the egg on her spoon, whilst wearing a microskirt and carrying all else before her. When the whistle blew she started off at such a fantastic pace that it was clear no one else would get anywhere near her. She cut the most wonderfully seductive figure but, at about the 50 metre point, the headmaster's father, who owned the school, let it be known that he felt rather differently about it as, indeed, did his wife who said extremely firmly and slightly fiercely to her son 'She must go!' I felt desperately sorry for her and for the headmaster whose secretary she was.

I had to give the prizes sometime after the egg and spoon race, but the heavens opened and I realised I would have to speak inside. No such luck. We were truly British and I stood there giving prizes and talking to the parents with water dripping off the end of my nose. Finally, we all stood to attention and sang the National Anthem and I thought how wonderful it is to be a teacher in the independent sector in England.

This was almost as alarming as my experience with the first secretary I appointed at Ellesmere. A delightful young lady applied who had been personal assistant to one of the directors of Fenwicks, the ladies dress store in Bond Street. I appointed her. She was very efficient but arrived every morning in a different outfit looking very glamorous indeed. I think she must have been given half the stock at Fenwicks when she left. My wife, however, was not so impressed. My shock came at the end of my first year as Headmaster when, on the last day of term, she announced her engagement to the Head Boy! I do hope that they are still happy. All my subsequent appointments were wonderful middle-aged ladies with families.

Preaching sermons is always likely to cause problems, one way or another. You are never quite sure where to sit, you always worry that you are going to get up and speak at the wrong moment or say precisely the wrong thing. One school I addressed held their services in such a beautiful chapel that I stood there, having processed in with the choir, and gazed at the beauty of the building. A senior pupil saw me standing there and, assuming that I did not know my way around the Book of Common Prayer, left her seat, presented me with the same book open at the right page and returned to hers. Possibly my worst experience was when I went to preach a sermon which contained a story about St Francis of Assisi. It involved my taking a pottery vase with me, which I intended to smash. As I was not very keen on breaking valuable vases, I took one from the school pottery, an early attempt by a boy that was about to be thrown away. It had a rather thick base but I had no idea how thick until I threw it over the edge of the pulpit to smash it on the tiles below. It should have been a dramatic gesture; it should have made my point more effectively than words as the shards scattered across the floor. Instead, this amazingly tough vase bounced off the floor and hit a small boy in the front pew on the head. The point of my sermon was, I believe, lost. One boy wrote in the school magazine that Mr Beer came to preach but that he was a vandal.

Once or twice, when giving prizes away, I have used two cabbages to illustrate my point. My wife had previously 'doctored' one of the cabbages so that it had no heart at all and these two vegetables represented two pupils. I would ask two pupils to come and tear off the leaves representing, as it were, marks in various subjects in the examination, whilst others represented games, music, drama, etc. One pupil ended up with nothing but a stalk, whilst the other still had a fine heart. This then gave me the opportunity to talk of the fruits of the spirit, honesty, compassion, integrity, whatever. I was reported in the magazine *Punch* as saying 'what we want at Ellesmere/ Lancing/ Harrow are pupils more like cabbages.' It is not possible to win against the media.

I believe that the different educational philosophies adopted by preparatory schools are one of the reasons for their success. They enable parents looking for something specific to find it amongst all this variety, as only variety absorbs variety. Two preparatory schools fairly close to each other give an excellent illustration of this. I went to one to give away the prizes and arrived, as requested, at 11 a.m. My wife and I were placed in seats on the sports field with the white posts and white cord in front of us. Music began to be played and the headmaster arrived at the front of his entire school as he marched them round the field. He was dressed as the old army PT sergeant might have been; plimsolls, white cricket panels, white vest with a badge. He was much older than I was, but he held himself wonderfully upright and he marched extremely smartly. Behind him came rows and rows of boys all dressed alike, all extremely smart and all marching in step brilliantly. They were lined up in rows of three in front of their guest of honour. They then began a series of PT exercises which were reminiscent of a Baden Powell camp, or army recruits in the First World War. They swung their arms, they punched the air, they performed knees bends and they sang. They sang all kinds of things and they sang to all the exercises. When they began to sing 'Ten Green Bottles' I realised I was in for a marathon that day. Eventually we had lunch whilst the boys had their sandwiches. I felt rather embarrassed as I tucked into smoked salmon and some rather sophisticatedly stuffed chicken. However, at 2 o'clock we were back in our chairs and the sports races began. Eventually, at 6 o'clock in the evening, I was asked to give away the prizes and make a speech. We returned home as fast as we could, as we were giving a dinner party, only to realise that the Wimbledon final between Borg and McEnroe had been going on for almost as long as we had been at sports that day!

In complete contrast, the school down the road held a very simple prize-giving. The school gathered. The headmaster said a very few words and then invited me to speak for no more than three minutes. He had not warned me. Thinking on my feet I gave a very rapid precis of what I had intended to say and managed to sit down exactly three minutes later. The headmaster then asked me to give away the prize, for there was but one. This did not go to an individual but to an entire House. He told the assembled company that the House which had come third (I forget the name), should come up and shake hands with their visitor. I did as I was told. The runner-up House was invited to do the same thing. Finally, the winning House came up and all shook me by the hand before one of their number carried away the prize. I, foolishly as it turned out, thought that I had done my task, but the headmaster then said that I would not wish to leave the school without shaking hands with every pupil and so would the fourth House now kindly come and meet their visitor. I always find it difficult to shake hands without talking very briefly to the individual concerned. This prizegiving therefore went on for a very long time and I was quite exhausted, but at least the headmaster had his wish, which was that every child should be treated in exactly the same way as every other child irrespective of his ability or attitude.

26

Punishments

THERE can be few more emotive subjects in a school than punishments. Most, but not all, teachers believe that there must be sanctions of one kind or another and, at least in the independent sector, formal punishments have been developed over a very long period of time and become traditional. I have already written about corporal punishment, in which I do not believe, but there are other forms of punishment, some of which might be judged as cruel, which have, to use the modern expression, 'passed their sell-by date.'

For example, when I became a young housemaster at Marlborough College in 1957 any boy who was senior by a term to any other boy could punish if the more junior were cheeky. The punishment consisted of running from the basement of the house to the top (it was four floors tall) and back again within a certain prescribed time. If the young man did not succeed in achieving this object he was made to do it again and again until he did. Obviously, the law of diminishing returns applied here and the punishment became a form of institutional bullying. I abolished it and also introduced my own form of punishment within the House. This nearly always involved scrubbing floors, cleaning windows or some other chore. Even this brought difficulties with it, for the houseman, who was paid to do such jobs, resented small boys doing what he considered his work.

The House I inherited was a Junior House and boys arrived straight from their preparatory schools, stayed with me usually for one year and then moved to their senior house. I thought it was a bad system, as I got to know the boys well, but by the time they left me they had, for the most part, gone into an adolescent silence which made it more difficult for the senior housemaster to understand them. When I left, I wrote a paper for the Master hoping that the system would be abolished. I believe that it now has been. The House was run as a copy of a senior House with prefects in charge. These prefects were only just senior to their charges and I did not believe that they were able to make important decisions at their age, and could not see why only a few boys should experience leadership. I wanted every boy to have the opportunity to accept responsibility and lead for a short time, and then to observe another of his peers attempting to carry out a comparable task. I therefore abolished the prefectorial system, and substituted a system whereby a task was organised by a boy who held the position for a month before giving it up and passing it on to another. In this way every boy experienced responsibility and no one became too big for his boots at that young age. During the year every boy held responsibility for something about three times. Unfortunately, my house was only part of a huge building and Dennis Silk, who was later to become a very distinguished Warden of Radley, was housemaster of the other part on the lower floor. He was not anxious to share this building with 'the communist state' that I was creating upstairs. We took my idea to the Master of Marlborough who agreed to let me reorganise the House, and Dennis had to put up with it. Dennis was, as usual, extremely generous in supporting me, even though he totally disagreed with what I was doing, and we coexisted happily for the rest of my time at Marlborough. My successor in the House, I am glad to say, kept the communist state going.

I always took the line that for the majority of pupils a punishment should be creative in one form or another. It could either be creative as far as the society was concerned, even if terrible for the boy being punished, or it could be a creative activity for the pupil himself. At Harrow, for example, I instituted the Head Master's punishment, which was sweeping the gutters in the roads over Harrow Hill. I did this because the Council was not very good at doing it, so it was very helpful to the community. As far as the boy was concerned it was an unpleasant task, the more especially because I insisted that it should be done very early in the morning.

That punishment was, I believe, fairly successful until the media heard about it. Moreover, they heard that a relation of Her Majesty the Queen was being punished in this way and nothing would have been more satisfactory for certain tabloid newspapers than to get a photograph. The boys and I played cat and mouse with the national press and we rather enjoyed it. When we could see the press photographers lurking around the Hill, the boys knew that they were excused the punishment for the morning. When the coast was clear they were back with their brooms and shovels. On this occasion we 'won' and no photographs were taken.

Individual creativity is sometimes useful for a young man the cause of whose misbehaviour is a lack of self-respect or belief that he is not respected by others, for example because he feels he cannot do anything well. Many is the time when I have asked for two or three pictures to be painted by the end of term, or something made in the technology department, or a piece of pottery completed, the execution of which has given the young man great satisfaction and pleasure. Some would not call this punishment, but if the effect is for the young man to find pride in himself, and then to behave properly, I believe it must be a valuable exercise. Others believe that an individual's talent should not be 'used' as his punishment. I sympathise with that, but do not necessarily agree.

On my first day at Harrow I was asked by a housemaster to see the father of a boy who was, apparently, being very difficult and doing little work. The housemaster told me that he thought the boy had too much pocket money. The father and I talked and I gently asked how much pocket money the boy was given. I cannot, now, remember the sum but it was greatly in excess of my own spending money for everyday wants. I said to the father that I felt we could solve the problem with the boy fairly easily. The father was intrigued and asked what I recommended. I said that I wanted the pocket money reduced by 80%. The father said that there would be no problem with that except . . . 'Who, Head Master, is going to tell my son?' I knew then that we had found the reason for the difficulty and so I said, 'I will be very happy to tell him provided you reduce the supply of money.' We agreed and he left. Later, I saw the boy and sat him down. 'I have bad news for you, which I fear is my doing' I said, 'your pocket is to be reduced, not by 10%, or even halved, but by 80%.' He looked at me and said 'Oh, Sir, thank you so much. I always hated having all that money.' He never looked back after that.

Some boys may be so disturbed or going through such a terrible phase in adolescence that they need firmer treatment. A few boys, whom I believed were emotionally disturbed, were sent with their parents' permission to a friary to be cared for by priests. Sometimes they found the discipline of getting up early, saying their prayers for an hour, a silent breakfast, and a service in chapel a routine which made school seem like a holiday camp. Several of these young men returned happily to school, helped also by the skill and understanding of the friars.

Sometimes one has to consider the community as a whole rather than just one individual. If an individual is causing so much disturbance that other pupils are beginning to behave badly as a result, then the so-called 'bad apple' must be removed for a while or, sadly, sometimes permanently. Rustication, the removal of a pupil for a short period of time, is a comparatively modern punishment. I believe it to be very valuable as it is a clear signal to the boy concerned that the community of which he is a part may not be prepared to allow him to stay there, unless he alters his behaviour sufficiently to make that possible. Parental reaction, however, can vary enormously.

Once I had a pupil whom I thought I might have to rusticate. I knew that his father might be difficult and, to be fair, he was not always in this country.

I therefore decided that it would be wise to warn both father and son that the next stage in handling the boy's behaviour could well be rustication. I knew the boy understood very well but I was not so sure about the father. How right I was! I received a postcard from a yacht somewhere in a sunnier climate, which read simply:

Dear Ian,
Thank you for your most unwelcome letter. May I remind you that I've paid for part of your salary to look after my son throughout the whole of the term time and under no circumstances will you ever return him home during that period. All good wishes,
Yours ever

In complete contrast, I think of another young man who was behaving badly whom I had also warned about possible rustication. This young man informed me that it would not be possible for me to rusticate him for the usual period of three days as he lived many thousands of miles away. I warned him that he should not try me out as I meant what I said. To my horror and sadness, he continued to behave badly and I was forced to rusticate him for three days. This meant one day travelling out, one day at home and one day travelling back. It was an expensive exercise and I had to be as sure of my ground as possible. I sent with the young man a letter to his father. When the boy returned I asked him what his father had said and the young man told me that he had said nothing. I was disappointed, as I thought the father was with me in demanding the highest standards. However, the boy handed me a letter from his father which read:

Dear Ian,
I do apologise for my son's behaviour. I have told him that I will not speak to him again until you have informed me that he is behaving like a proper English gentleman.
Yours ever

I am glad to say that both these young men grew up well and, as far as I know, are still doing fine.

Sometimes it is necessary to do the reverse of rustication namely, to request the presence of the father in the headmaster's study. On one occasion I did this when the father was literally on the other side of the world. The boy informed me that under no circumstances would his father travel to see me simply because of his son's behaviour. I knew that if the father did travel, the young man would almost certainly behave properly as he would be so amazed that his father loved him enough to make such a sacrifice. Needless to say, I was extremely worried about the strategy, but I did persuade the father to travel and the boy's astonishment when they met each other in my study twenty-four hours later was amazing. It did the trick and the boy progressed, happy in his newly-found security.

The love of the parent for the child can be so overwhelming as to cause problems of its own. One new boy, whose mother lived fairly near the school, insisted on coming to the school at about six every evening to put hot water bottles in the boy's bed. I was not aware of this practice until the housemaster telephoned me to say that things had become impossible and the boy was being teased mercilessly. I asked the housemaster to ask the mother to come to my house for sherry after she had placed the hot water bottles. She duly arrived and, having given her a glass of sherry, told her that she had problem. She had either to take the boy away there and then or she would accept my expulsion from the school. 'What do you mean by that', she said. I told her that she would not be allowed into the school until I gave her permission. There were lots of tears but, to her credit, she accepted the discipline on herself and left the boy alone. The following term I reinstated her and we never looked back.

The most extraordinary experience I had punishing someone followed a letter I received from a boy confessing theft from a house changing room. Apparently the housemaster had asked the culprit to own up but he had not done so. Instead he wrote to me, confessing the crime and asking me to punish and forgive him. I did both, but the thief had waited forty-five years to confess as he was aged sixty when he wrote to me! I adjusted the sum he had stolen for inflation and suggested he send me a cheque for his chosen charity. This he did and I went to chapel to ask for his forgiveness.

The worst decision that a headmaster ever has to take is to expel or exclude a pupil; it is a nightmare. The moment when you know that you will lose the confidence of the other teachers, the confidence of the other pupils, and the confidence of their parents, if you allow a particular individual to continue to stay in the community, is the moment when you know you have to ask the parents to take him or her away. I do not like the word expulsion; it is old-fashioned. The pupil is asked to leave to begin another life at another school where he or she can be more successful. The judgment one has to make is very difficult. No one knows whether you get it right or not. In my experience, on the occasions when I had decided not to expel and to give the pupil the benefit of the doubt, I was nearly always proved wrong. Almost invariably the pupil had to go eventually but had simply created more unhappiness and further damaged himself and others during the extra time I had given him.

Explaining to parents what you intend to do is a ghastly experience but, provided the welfare of the pupil you are removing is always your first priority, the parents concerned can possibly understand. It always means finding an alternative school for the pupil as quickly as possible so that a career is less interrupted. Fortunately the independent sector is such a comparatively small club that it is possible to try and identify the right school for a pupil you are removing. It is understood that you can ask a colleague whether he will give the student a second chance. Every head has experienced this situation and I believe it to be one of the strengths of the independent sector that pupils can be moved in this way. The pupil who was unhappy and therefore behaving badly and not succeeding in one school can quite often be moved to another and become a huge success. That is what you hope and pray will happen when you remove a child and, indeed, when you accept one from another school. On occasion I have asked a senior pupil, whom I have asked to leave the school, if he would like to return when he is older, have lunch as a symbol that all is forgotten and consider joining the old boys association. This has always been successful. One or two of the pupils whom I asked to leave one of the schools that I have been responsible for do nevertheless remain on my conscience.

27

Teaching

I PRESUME that everyone who goes into teaching enjoys teaching lessons. At least to begin with. I fell in love with the idea of teaching when I was in the school in Abergele in North Wales and fell for the biology mistress, Miss Lloyd. She inspired me with a love for biology; the North Wales countryside excited me with its combination of mountains, rivers and seashore, and in those days we had the freedom to roam. Birdwatching, fishing and searching the shoreline became my pastimes at the age of nine. These were the days before it was realised that egg collecting was wrong, and I had a very fine collection. Miss Lloyd dissected a rabbit for me after lessons and, in return, I wrote her a book about the rabbit.

I was further inspired at my secondary school, Whitgift in South Croydon, by a brilliant botanist, Dr Cecil Prime, who became the leading authority on *Arum maculatum* or Lords and Ladies, as it is often called. I gained an Exhibition to St Catharine's College, Cambridge, in March 1949 and had one more term at school before joining the army to do my National Service for two years. I was invited by the Headmaster and Dr Prime to teach biology to the younger pupils at Whitgift. I leapt at the chance and had the most wonderful time preparing my lessons, teaching and marking. I did not think I had ever been so happy and I learnt more about how to teach then than I did when I studied for my Post Graduate Certificate of Education.

At Cambridge I was working in a laboratory, drawing plant cells, when the lecturer watched me carefully for about five minutes. He then said, 'Were you a boy at Whitgift?' 'Yes, I was,' I said 'but how did you guess?' The lecturer said, 'You were taught by Cecil Prime. He is the only man in the country who knows how to teach pupils how to draw plant cells!' I thought to myself how wonderful it must be to be such a fine teacher that your pupils can be recognised by the work they do.

I really had no doubt about being a teacher despite the fact that I was tempted by a scholarship to Paris University to take a PhD studying protozoa and another to go to St Mary's Hospital to train as a doctor. Instead, I was interviewed and offered jobs by about five independent schools. I think the

Colonel Ross Beckett OBE, officer commanding the Harrow CCF, with
Major General Cosmo Nevill CB, CBE, DSO, ex Colonel of the Royal Fusiliers, Old Harrovian.

Harrow, 1990. The author, assisted by Caspar de Bono, starts the Ducker run to Marble Arch and back
to raise money for charity.

Mrs Beer and the ladies of the Herga Committee raise money for charity at a Donkey Derby on 5 May 1990.

The Harrow School show jumping team win the inter Service competition at the Windsor Horse Show and receive their rosettes from Her Majesty the Queen.

Harrow. School Bill. The Head Master takes Bill, supported by the Head of School, James Rous.

Harrow. Annual party for the monitors after their training course before the beginning of term.

Prize Giving to the Jewish Class at Harrow. The Head Master presents the books to prize winners, whilst their teacher, Dr Freund, looks on.

Harrow. Founders Day, Dinner and Songs, March 1991. Included in the photograph are: The Rt Revd Michael Mann, Chairman of Governors (*back row, left*), Lord Butler (*back row, third from left*), Head of School James Rous (*front row, second from left*) and, moving right, Mrs Beer, the author and another ex Head of School, Andrew Butler.

Mr Michael Noakes, PPPROI, RP, paints the author's portrait in his study.

Harrow, February 1991. Singing our farewell 'We said we wouldn't look back' from *Salad Days* at the 'Fabulous Fifties' concert organised by the Harrow ladies to raise money for local charities.

Harrow, 28 June 1991. The last day of term, and of the author's schoolmastering career, is honoured by HRH Princess Margaret.

'Here, Sir!' The farewell gift to the author by the boys of the school.

arrow, 28 June
91. Road closed
farewell.

4 June 1994. South Africa v. England in Pretoria. England won 32–15. Singing 'God save the Queen' with President Mandela and Vice President de Clerk before the game.

The launch of the GTC. *Left to right*: the oldest member (the author), the youngest (Usha Devi), the minister (Estelle Morris), the chief executive (Carol Adams) and the chairman (Lord Puttnam)

reason for this was that, while studying for my PGCE at Cambridge, I did my teaching practice at Wellington College in Berkshire. It was known that I was, as it were, 'on the market' and, whilst I had never been in a boarding school before I was greatly attracted by the ethos of such an establishment. On the one hand, I wanted to teach in the maintained sector and throw stones at the independent sector which I felt was too exclusive. On the other, I thought it would be fun to go to an independent boarding school and try changing things from the inside. I therefore accepted the job which gave me the poorest salary (£300 per annum plus board and lodging in term time) but offered me the richest experience in a brilliant biology department led by Sir Francis Knowles, who later became a Professor and a Fellow of the Royal Society. The school was Marlborough College in Wiltshire. Sir Francis was something of an eccentric. He owned an Elizabethan manor and carried out research into the neurons between the eyes of prawns which mated in May only in the Bay of Naples. What a wise man he was to have such a specialised research project. He inspired me and gave me a great deal of freedom as a teacher.

His first decision was to allow me to teach five Oxbridge candidates in the term after they had passed their A-level biology, or rather their A-levels in botany and zoology. They were very bright pupils and I taught them once a week at 9 o'clock in the evening in my study. I really enjoyed those lessons; I spent a long-time preparing them and challenging the boys in advance of their Oxbridge scholarships. At the end of the term, they gave me a small gift and one said 'Sir, we have really enjoyed this term but we do think we should tell you that we have not understood a single thing you have been saying!' An important lesson. How often, since then, have I seen enthusiastic young teachers aiming too high for the pupils they teach.

I also learned another lesson that first term. Apparently, someone had damaged a microscope and it was known to be a pupil in the lower sixth. There were two large sets and I was teaching the less bright group. I was told by Sir Francis that I had to fine each boy a certain sum of money in order to repair the microscope as no one had owned up to being the perpetrator of the damage. I remember vividly telling the form this news at the end of a practical dissection class. There was silence and then one boy said, 'If you think we are going to pay up, you have another think coming!' I could hardly believe my ears and, irrationally, said 'If any of you are left in my laboratory after thirty seconds I shall knock you through the wall!' Probably one of the more ridiculous comments I have ever made to a group of boys. Today, the Ofsted inspector would condemn me out of hand. The boys all paid up, but I thought I should mention the rudeness of this one boy to his housemaster.

To my horror, I learnt that the boy had received four strokes of the cane for impertinence. He then came to visit me to apologise. I asked him why he had spoken as he had and the simple answer was 'You are a new teacher, someone had to try you out and I was the one who was elected. It didn't work!' From that day on I have never ever had any trouble with any form I have ever taught.

More salutary still was my short experience teaching chemistry. The head of science at Marlborough asked if I would take one form for chemistry as the chemistry department was short of teachers. I hated the idea but could not really avoid the challenge. All went reasonably well until I took that well-known lesson on the preparation of oxygen. I had mixed potassium chloride and manganese dioxide in a large boiling tube. I heated up a mixture and collected the oxygen in jars over water; the bee-hive I think it is called. I collected about five jars of oxygen, and then carried out various demonstrations with the whole class clustering around the demonstration bench. Looking back, how I could have allowed them altogether round at the front of the bench and at each end, I simply do not know. Ofsted would have failed me a second time. However, what the inspector would have said to the next part of my lesson I dread to think. I needed one more cylinder of oxygen, so I reheated the mixture in the large boiling tube. It began to glow red, gave off very little oxygen and then surprised us all by exploding. It exploded most satisfactorily. The back end of the boiling tube hit the child on my right and the bottom of his tie fell off. The contents of the tube hit the child at the end of the bench on my left where small holes appeared in his shirt. To this day I thank God that none got anywhere near his face, especially his eyes. Naturally, the boys were hugely delighted. 'Oh! Sir! Please do it again!'

The head of chemistry rebuked me afterwards, treating my lack of knowledge about the effects of reheating potassium chloride and manganese dioxide as evidence of insanity. However, it had the desired effect and I was taken off chemistry teaching.

This decision gave me more time to indulge in my love for ecology. It was a comparatively new aspect of the biology curriculum in those days, but it allowed sixth form pupils to study on their own with project work. We were most fortunate that next to the laboratories were ancient water meadows. No one at Marlborough, at that time, knew much about their workings and we spent about three years on various projects involving mapping the original water courses and then looking carefully at the distribution of animals such as snails, leeches and other freshwater invertebrates. The mapping began by persuading the services to take us up in a helicopter to photograph from the air. We were amazed at the detail which was observable at a low height. Undulations in the ground not visible at eye level became prominent from the helicopter. Two of my pupils, J. D. Leatherdale and R. H. L. Disney, published this work in the Marlborough College Natural History Society Reports 1957. I am very pleased they did so, as the water meadows are no more, now built on or levelled for playing fields. In the following two years excellent work was completed and published in the same Journal by two more sixth form pupils: D. L. Formby on the distribution of flatworms in the water meadows and J. V. B. Robinson on polymorphism in snails on the Marlborough Downs.

Formal appraisal of teaching was unheard of when I began my career. You sank or you swam. I had never found maintaining discipline difficult but I had found it difficult to pitch the individual lesson at the right level for the pupils I was teaching. I always worried that, even when I felt I had it right, there would be one or two who would be bored or simply would not understand. And, of course, they rarely told you. I wanted to create a classroom with three buttons on every desk, red, green and amber. Each individual could signal to the master control set on my desk whether he wanted me to go on (green), wanted to ask a question (amber) or was simply fed up with the lesson, had heard the joke before, or did not understand (red). I discussed the idea with pupils and colleagues, I even wrote an article about it, but never put it into practice. I had this vision of a head with the master control in his study, so that at any one moment he could tell whether all the pupils in the school were being properly taught or not!

I used to talk through such ideas with the Master of Marlborough, Tommy Garnett, an inspiring man. Eventually I had a note from him informing me that he had decided to come and listen to me teaching and would I suggest an appropriate lesson for him to observe. I decided to ask him to come to a Lower Sixth group who were not scientists but had opted for a course on human physiology. I felt that as he was not a scientist he might be more interested in the general study of the subject. I had completed a great deal of the theory and had decided to dissect a rat in front of the class, so that they could see something of the organs and systems that we had only discussed in theory.

I was worried that the rat would be too small for everyone to see clearly and the rats were in any case always colourless, having been kept in preservative. There was nothing else on offer. By chance I was telephoned the evening before the Master was due to come to my lesson by the master of the beagle pack. He told me that one of the beagles had died suddenly and asked whether I would be prepared to carry out an autopsy. I said I knew little about diseases of dogs but he told me he only wanted to know whether there was anything unusual about the animal before he had it buried. I agreed to have a look and the Master of Marlborough found himself watching one of his young teachers dissecting a beagle for the class. I had never dissected such a large animal before and it was very hard work. Sweat dropped into thoracic and abdominal cavities as I slaved away with inappropriate instruments. For an hour and a half I worked, explaining to the class all the details of the organs, blood vessels, nerves and so on that they had seen in pictures but never in reality. The beagle proved to be a good demonstration animal, but I found nothing wrong with it, other than the fact that it had been presented to me dead.

At the end of the lesson the Master took me on one side and I had my fingers crossed. 'Amazing, extraordinary, never seen anything like it before. Oh dear . . . oh dear . . .' and, like the White Rabbit in *Alice in Wonderland*, he wandered off muttering to himself, never to speak of it again. His revenge came when Angela and I were staying with him at their holiday home in Suffolk. Two dogs decided to procreate their race in full view of everyone in the centre of their garden. One of their small children said 'Daddy, what are they doing?' And the Master of Marlborough very quickly said 'Oh, Mr Beer knows all about that. He will tell you' and walked off.

Those were the days when it was expected that you could teach thirty-four periods out of thirty-six on the timetable, run rugby football for the College, be a House Tutor, an Officer in the CCF, coach hockey and, as far as I was concerned, run the swimming in the summer term. Now there was more to the latter than anyone today might expect. The pool was outdoor and was a concrete-lined moat around the old mound in the centre of the College grounds. It was said to be one of the biggest outdoor pools in the country. At the age of twenty-four, and with all my other duties, I was the sole adult in charge of cleaning the pool after the winter, of filling it and then hand-chlorinating it before organising a rota to supervise swimming every day throughout the summer term. To clean the pool I asked about thirty thirteen-year-olds to come down in the afternoon and sweep the pool clean while I tried to operate an old pump from the side of the deep end of the pool. It required a lot of discipline to get the boys with their brooms to sweep side by side across the width of the pool and walk down the length. It took about four days to clean and about three days to fill up. We then poured in the chlorine from glass vats, which were embedded in straw in iron surrounds. One year a boy poured the liquid in the deep end and the glass vat slipped out of its container. It broke and we had to empty the pool and start again.

Once the pool was in use I had to get up before seven each morning and hand-chlorinate all round the edge of the pool using a watering can. After about six weeks of this my track suit bottom had been bleached and then rotted off, so I went to the Bursar to ask the College to pay for a replacement. No such luck. I cleaned and maintained that pool for my entire five years at Marlborough. I suppose it was good training for my headmastership.

At one stage a bottle of hydrogen cyanide was stolen from the laboratories and the Master sent for me one Friday evening to give me this information in the strictest confidence. He told me he was deeply worried lest the culprit poured it into the pool and that I must immediately turn on the water and wash it out. The new water was, of course, very cold and we had arranged all the swimming fixtures a few weeks after the pool was originally filled, hoping that the sun would warm the contents up a little. The following day was our first school fixture but I had no choice other than to turn on the water and tell no-one. Early on the Saturday morning the captain of swimming rushed into my study 'Sir! Some maniac has turned on the water in the pool.' 'Yes', I said, 'it was me. I thought that if the water were really cold then, when you dived in, you would swim faster than ever before to get to the other end and out.' 'We have thought for some time', he said, 'that you were mad and now I know you really are!' I was not able to tell him the truth until three days later when the cyanide was found.

Around this time I began to think that I ought to leave independent education and join the maintained sector. The division between the two irritated me and I could not see how the barriers could be broken down as so much money would be required. It seemed to me irrelevant that the independent schools saved the country much money by parents paying, as it were, twice over. The fact that the schools gave away much more money than they gained through tax concessions I conveniently ignored and felt I should go into the mainstream. Donald Wright, then a housemaster at Marlborough, later Headmaster of Shrewsbury and subsequently the Archbishops' Appointments Secretary, was sympathetic to my cause. He introduced me to Harry Rée, then Headmaster of Watford Grammar School. I asked Harry if I could go and stay with him to see whether I really wanted to change. I then found that my abilities, whatever they were, were really best suited to boarding rather than day education, although I had always been ambivalent about boarding itself. Before I had time to work it all out I met Angela, was offered Ellesmere and was caught up in the system forever. Nevertheless, it partly explains why, as Chairman of HMC, I was the first to ask the President of the Secondary Heads Association to read the lesson at our annual service. That year it was Molly Hattersley. It also explains why the *Times Educational Supplement* stated in 1989 'Other ambitions still won't leave him alone. "I'd like to see a staff college for heads. And a general teaching council." Hold on, isn't running a school supposed to exhaust people?' Little did I believe that I would see the former created and that I would sit on the latter.

I was fortunate, at that time, to be invited to take a Rugby Football XV of Oxford and Cambridge Blues to play in Paris on one Sunday each year against Paris University Club. For once in my life I became quite popular with my contemporaries who all wanted to come. On one occasion I selected the team including a Marlborough housemaster and colleague, Dennis Silk, and decided to complete the team with my two other good friends at Marlborough. Maurice Gray, who was to become the chaplain at Ellesmere in due course, was to be the touch judge and our dentist, Bryn Evans, came as a manager.

I had not asked permission of the Master, Tommy Garnett, as I had no intention that we should miss any of our duties in the College. Dennis and I were taking school rugby matches on the Saturday afternoon and, when we had completed them, we drove to Heathrow to catch an aeroplane to Paris. We arrived late that Saturday evening and had a very good dinner and party. We slept late on Sunday morning, played the match on Sunday afternoon and were then given a fine French banquet to celebrate the game. We caught an aeroplane very late that evening to fly back to Heathrow.

As we approached Heathrow the plane was turned round, due to fog, and returned to Paris. By this time it was about three o'clock in the morning. We persuaded our dentist, the so-called manager, to telephone the Master early in the morning and explain that three of his masters were marooned in Paris and did not expect to return to College until late on Monday. The Master, of course, had no idea we were there and we all had full teaching programmes that day.

We returned to Marlborough College at about six in the evening, weighed down with bottles of various types of liquid to pacify our various colleagues who had had to teach our lessons. Needless to say, I was sent to the Master to explain all.

It turned out that he was ill in bed with a cold. I was summoned into his bedroom where he had just been reading the write-up of the match which had been reported, much to my surprise, in *The Times* on the Monday morning.

'I see you won the match', he said. 'Yes, Master' I said. 'I saw you running the first XV on Saturday afternoon. When did you leave?' he asked. I explained what we had done and what had happened. He listened.

And then he said 'You could not have had much sleep on Saturday night, and clearly you had a very tough game on Sunday afternoon followed by a celebration dinner and so you did not sleep on Sunday night. Is that true?' I confirmed it was true. 'I know you will be on a CCF night scheme tomorrow night and playing for the County the following day', he continued. 'Yes, Master', I mumbled. 'Then you will be a very tired young man by Thursday morning', he said and indicated that I should leave his bedroom.

He even put up with me taking my Young Leaders Platoon to circle his house and then kidnap the boy head of the Combined Cadet Force as he left the Master's Lodge after a meeting there. We then took this young man up into the Downs for the night, so that he would not be on parade the following morning for the annual field day exercise. We wanted to see whether it was true that orders had been delegated downwards and that his absence on parade would make no difference. However, as we had to get him back on parade at some time during the morning, we had to obtain his uniform from his dormitory. I recall following a young man, Rupert McGuigan, now a Secretary in the Royal Household, over the rooftops of 'C' House in the College and climbing in through the upper window of a dormitory. Everything went like clockwork and my Young Leaders Platoon was brilliant. What was not so good was the fact that we proved our point. The orders had not been delegated, the field day began in chaos and I was, quite rightly, extremely unpopular with my fellow officers. Nevertheless I was still supported by the Master.

I enjoyed teaching so much that, despite the fact that I was appointed to be a headmaster at the early age of 29, I taught A-level biology in all the three schools I headmastered. The plan did come to something of a halt at Harrow. I appointed a new head of department, Richard Burden, a young biologist whom I greatly admired. He came to see me during the summer term to discuss my teaching programme for the next year. He very politely explained that, as the biology department had expanded, there were more assistant masters who wanted to teach the sixth form and he wondered whether I would mind stepping down. He added, as an aside, 'I think probably, Head Master, that the subject has changed so greatly in recent years that you might feel happier not teaching at A-level. However,' he continued 'we all know how you like a challenge and therefore I would like you to teach the bottom set for GCSE. This will not only give you an idea of the weaker boys coming into the school, but it will mean that you will be retrained to understand and tackle GCSE which is, I am sure, exactly what you would like in order to keep up to date.' I roared with laughter. 'I knew' I said 'that I had appointed the right person to run the department. Do with me as you wish.' And that was the end of the sixth form, although I was still teaching some general studies at that level. The experience of teaching GCSE biology was invaluable.

I always thoroughly enjoyed teaching sixth form general studies as I felt biology had, for too long, been a cinderella subject. I used to have groups of boys from the classical or history sixth who might have done very little biology before, and try to excite them about my subject. As I felt strongly that biology was going to be the subject for the 21st century I had much with which to challenge them. For example, future knowledge of how the brain worked, the discoveries that were becoming inevitable in genetics and the explosion that would take place in ecology and environmental studies meant that there was much to talk about. Because many of them felt it a bore to miss their specialised subjects and study sciences, which they had tried hard to avoid, I had to whet their appetite in order to excite them about the subject. On one occasion I perhaps went too far and evidently worried one boy about an issue which is now commonplace. I cannot now recall whether the subject was cloning, choosing the sex of your child, the manipulation of DNA, or the use of neurotransmitters as drugs. At the end of the lesson all the pupils left, bar one. He was a sensitive and highly intelligent young man who was a deeply committed Christian. His message for me, when we were on our own, was simple. 'I never wish to be taught another lesson by you ever again! You are evil!'. We had some discussion about the reasons for my lesson, and the reasons for his unhappiness and rejection of what I was saying. Eventually I think he understood that I was not evil and that I was simply trying to open their eyes. He burst into tears, grabbed the handkerchief which was in my top left-hand jacket pocket, wiped his eyes with it, blew his nose, put it back into my jacket pocket and left the room. Later, we became very good friends and I have one of his excellent watercolours hanging on a wall in our house to this day.

Trying to keep teaching commitments as a headmaster was not easy then and today I believe it to be near impossible. My happiest time teaching was the period just before I became a headmaster. I had an excellent group of sixth form biologists and was very anxious to take them on some kind of ecological survey. I was very fortunate to meet, quite accidentally, the owner of Tanera Mor, the largest of the Summer Isles off the west coast of Scotland, just north of Ullapool. Tanera Mor was written about in Fraser Darling's book 'Island Farm'. He farmed there during the war. There are now once again people living on the island, but when we visited it was uninhabited. I was given permission to take this group of seven pupils to live there for ten days if I could find the necessary funding. I was at that time an officer in the CCF and all the boys were cadets in the same unit. I therefore made an application through the CCF for funding to support an expedition to the island. This was granted and we had a most wonderful experience trying to live on this deserted island whilst carrying out an ecological survey. Every evening at 6 o'clock the old zoo man who used to speak on the BBC, Mr Seth Smith, had his telescope focused on the island in case we were in trouble. We agreed to light a bonfire if we needed help, and the coastguards had given us flares to set off in the event of any crisis. There were no problems and the 'boys' have just held a reunion for all of us, with our wives, forty years on. The 'boys' were approaching sixty but looking fit; three doctors, one army officer, one farmer and a television producer. The seventh, a doctor, sadly died several years before the reunion.

The point of the story, however, concerns the CCF which I had always felt should be more involved with outward bound challenges, such as mine to Tanera Mor, and less with drill on the parade ground. All was well until the annual inspection of the CCF. I was told that the inspecting officer would wish to see how the nation's money had been spent on our expedition. I was delighted. We placed tents and methods of cooking our food on the lawns outside the biology laboratories while inside the laboratories we created a sort of biological model of Tanera Mor. This involved a lot of microscopes and some live specimens. When the inspecting officer came round he was not as interested as I had anticipated. Indeed, he was rather cross and demanded to know what all this had got to do with the army. I attempted to explain and thought I might have got through. I realised about a fortnight later that I had not when I was summoned to see the officer commanding the CCF, who asked me for my resignation. I could hardly believe my ears. Naturally, I refused to relinquish my commission, and the battle with the War Office began. I often wonder what the outcome would have been had I not shortly afterwards been appointed a headmaster. This allowed me to sidestep the problem, as a headmaster does not serve as an officer in his own CCF.

My very last lesson was taught on my very last day at Harrow just before I was due to welcome Princess Margaret to the school. The lesson was something to do with human physiology and the pupils were in their first year studying for GCSE. I remember asking a boy to come down to the front of the lecture room and demonstrate with me some function or other of the human frame. At the end of this highly successful experiment I playfully pushed the lad in jest. To my horror, either my strength had not diminished over the thirty-six years I had been teaching, or else the boy was a little off balance, or perhaps both. He fell backwards, hit his head on the laboratory bench and was helped to the medical centre. Shortly after, I rang the house matron and had a word with her and she told me that the boy was lying down but would probably survive. I could see my glorious career ending in disaster and I took it upon myself to telephone the parents, confess all and plead that my enthusiasm for teaching was undiminished even on the last day of my career! Thankfully they took it all in good part and I am only glad that the young man had a tough cranium.

28

Governors

LITTLE mention is made of the governors of independent schools unless the relationship with the head goes wrong, when the subsequent difficulties can sometimes reach the national newspapers. The role of the governors has changed a very great deal over the last forty years, but one aspect of the task has always been the same. Their relationship with their head has to be of the very highest order, and one of their first priorities must be to care for him or her and any family the he or she may have.

No head can operate properly if the governors show suspicion or lack of confidence in his or her ability. The position of the head, particularly in a boarding school, is an extremely lonely one. The head's family is in constant social contact with all the other families involved with the school. Yet all these families know that it is the head who hires and fires. However much they may wish to, it is not really possible for a head or his wife to make special friends until they leave.

Throughout my career I was extremely lucky with my governors, although my first contact with a governor was not very encouraging. I was doing my term's experience at Wellington College while I was studying for my Post Graduate Certificate of Education at Cambridge. One Sunday afternoon I went training with a rugby ball as I was then playing for England and I took three members of the 1st XV with me who wanted some exercise. While we were out on the fields a man walking his dog came over to ask what I was doing. I explained. He then reported me to the Master of Wellington for taking games with boys on a Sunday afternoon. He was General Sir Claude Auchinleck, one of our most distinguished Second World War commanders.

We met our first Chairman of Governors socially after my appointment to Ellesmere but before we took up the position. The amazing and frightening Colonel Story had invited us to stay with him so that we could meet the Chairman of the Governors and his wife for an informal talk. We dressed for dinner and came down into the drawing-room to meet the Chairman's wife, Lady Offley Wakeman, who was on her own. She was very charming and began a conversation with us, treating us both as if we were even younger than our birth certificates claimed. At that stage I was twenty-nine years of age and my wife twenty-four. I was beginning to wonder what was going on when the Chairman, Sir Offley, entered the drawing-room and said 'My Dear, I am so glad that you have met our new Headmaster and his wife.' It then transpired that she thought we were the son and daughter of our host, Colonel Story; one still at university and the other at school!

My relationship with Sir Offley Wakeman was extremely friendly but rather distant. His charming wife gave Sunday lunches with some regularity and we went to their home to meet the gentry of North Shropshire. He assumed that I knew how to run the school and simply let me get on with it hoping that I would not have to bother him. He was very open to suggestions and, when I suggested two new governors, he readily agreed. They were both friends of mine as we had studied Natural Sciences together at Cambridge. Dr David Harrison, later Sir David and Master of Selwyn College, Cambridge, and Father Peter Ball, the founder with his twin brother of the Society of The Glorious Ascension. Both brothers later became Bishops. They were two people to whom I knew I could talk in confidence and with complete frankness—the greatest help to any head.

When I was invited to be Head Master of Lancing College in Sussex, I asked whether my two friends could come with me as they too were moving closer to Lancing. My new Chairman of Governors, Sir Charles Chadwyck Healey, readily agreed, and his support made my life so much easier in my new school. Sir Charles, or Cherry, as he was known to all his friends, could not have been more helpful. He understood the need to support not only me, but also my wife and children, and almost became an extra 'Uncle' to the family. If I ever wanted him, he immediately dropped all he was doing at home or work and would come straight over to Lancing. He was, however, much more demanding than Sir Offley, and I knew that he would be producing ideas constantly to challenge me. I found his company most stimulating. He also encouraged the other governors to involve themselves as closely as possible with the work of the school. Partly as a result of this, one of the other governors, Lord Cunliffe, gave up a week of his holiday to become a student in the College. He attended all lessons, Chapel and extra curricular activities and in every way became a full-time student. The detailed report he later wrote was challenging and stimulating for the rest of the governors to read and for myself to act upon.

When I moved to Harrow I was concerned that I might not have the same relationship with the governors there as I had had in my first two schools. I need not have worried as the quality of the governors, and their attitude towards their Head Master, could not have been faulted. They were deeply concerned about my happiness and that of my family; all else flowed from that. Amongst their number was Donald Lindsey whom I had admired for many years. He had not only been responsible for inspiring Malvern at a time when that school led the way in science education under John Lewis, but had also done a great deal for the arts there. He had been elected a governor of Harrow to represent the views of the masters and he was a constant guide and help to me as well as being the man responsible for enticing me to Harrow in the first place.

The Chairman, the Dean of Windsor, Michael Mann, made it very clear to me at the outset that he would always be available to me, day or night, should I need him. But if I did not, he had no intention of interfering with my running of the school and he would get on with his own professional work. The experience of working with Michael Mann is too recent for individual events to be recorded but his support for all that I tried to do was invaluable. When I requested that he took a strong line he took an even stronger one. When I respectfully suggested that he should be told of something but take no action, he accepted my advice. He was totally and utterly supportive of all that I tried to do.

There were also many other Governors at Harrow who loved their school and who supported the Head Master throughout. They were influential, intelligent and very busy men and women and I knew that if I ever let them down they would, discreetly, tell me precisely what they thought of me and where I was going wrong.

Michael Mann was eventually replaced by Sir Robin Butler, now Lord Butler, then the Cabinet Secretary. He had previously been our Chairman of Finance and taught me a great deal about handling the finances of a major institution. By chance his son, Andrew, arrived at Harrow as a thirteen-year-old the same term I arrived as the new Head Master. He later became Head of the School and I will never forget that morning at the beginning of his fifth year at Harrow when he entered my study and said 'Sir, we are all Beer's boys now.' Any headmaster will understand what that comment implied and it gave me a great deal of confidence. Meanwhile his father, with his lack of pomposity, clear brain and constant consideration for other people, was an example to us all. Harrow was extremely fortunate and, in a way, I was the beneficiary. For example, he agreed that I should present him with a precis of the minutes of Governors' Meetings the moment the meeting finished so that he could correct anything I had written. The minutes were then posted on my noticeboard in the Masters' Room within a half an hour of the meeting for all to read. This prevented a lot of rumour and gossip whilst keeping everyone in touch with management issues.

Amongst the governors were many who became friends. I have emphasised time and again at conferences and training courses that it is vital that governors include their own head amongst their friends and share something of their own personal expertise in business or professional life with him or her. Few did this better for me than Roger Boissier, Lady Soames, Evelyn de Rothschild, Geoffrey Simmonds (a governor in the USA) and Sir Michael Connell, the current Chairman.

All this meant that I really looked forward to governors' meetings, enjoying the company of the governors and knowing no one else could bother me while I was working with them.

The Harrow governors were accustomed to meet on Saturday mornings, but arrived at 4 p.m. on the previous day. This enabled them to hold an informal meeting with me on the Friday when I could discuss my report openly, frankly and with no minute taking. Problems were all sorted out at that meeting and any decisions were reported, formally, on Saturday morning. It also meant that the governors could dine in the school together with housemasters and assistant masters and their ladies, and senior boys. This helped to create a coherent and supportive Harrow team. The governors then stayed the night in masters' residences so that they could experience for themselves the conditions in which they had placed their masters and their families, as all lived in school property. I allowed masters to offer hospitality on Friday evening to specific governors and soon learned which were the most popular.

I sat as a governor on three HMC schools and a large number of preparatory schools, but my two favourites were Wellesley House School in Broadstairs, and Windlesham House in Sussex. The Wellesley governors usually met in Boodles and, after an aperitif, dined together, finishing with port which came round with the agenda. The papers had previously been sent to us and it was assumed we had all done our homework. The meeting was slick and efficient, and chaired by Robin Leigh-Pemberton in masterly fashion. The school thrived, was immensely happy and successful and so were the governing body. At Windlesham, in complete contrast, we nearly always met in the school and held our meeting before the delicious dinner prepared by Elizabeth Ann Malden who, together with Charles Malden, led what was in the seventies and eighties probably the most successful preparatory school in the country. Can there ever have been a more dynamic and progressive duo in the preparatory school world? I doubt it. Very sadly, Charles died early in retirement but left a legacy of hundreds of successful and happy young men and women who were greatly influenced by him.

I just hope that the increased bureaucracy with which all schools are now faced does not take away the opportunity to make friendships and have fun. If the bureaucracy gets much worse it will be more difficult to attract governors of high calibre to serve our schools. Maybe it is the responsibility of the independent school governors to persuade the government to reduce the bureaucracy for their colleagues in the maintained sector. If the independent schools had to cope with some of the pressures placed on the maintained sector, then many very distinguished men and women on the governing bodies of the independent schools would refuse to take office. The governors of all our schools must be trusted by governments, both local and national, to raise standards without endless form-filling. It is all to do with personal relationships—not paper.

29

❦❦❦❦❦❦❦❦❦❦❦❦❦❦❦❦❦❦❦❦❦❦❦❦

A Hobby

VERY early on in my teaching career I realised that coaching or teaching rugby football was closer to my heart than actually continuing to play. During my first term at Marlborough in 1955 I arranged for the 1st XV to tour in France at the end of term. We were the first major school to go on such a tour. I led the England pack in the Final trial at Twickenham on the Saturday and then flew out to Paris to catch up with the boys' team which had travelled earlier by ferry. When I reached them I found to my horror that my French was so poor that the club we were playing had assumed we were a university simply because we were called a College. The boys were due to play the adult team on the Sunday afternoon and, because my name was associated with the tour, they had imported a French international wing threequarter to strengthen their side. The Marlborough captain asked me to play and lead the side. I said I would play and lead the forwards, but that he must captain the side.

The band played before the game and when it came to the national anthems I glanced around the field to see the Marlborough boys standing as if they were just about to win their first Caps. They played 'out of their skins' and just won. The mayor gave a reception for them and, knowing by now that they were only boys, the town gave them a fantastic welcome and party. I did have some problems with the alcohol!

On the Monday I received the news I had been expecting; I had been dropped from the England team. My mind had been elsewhere and from then on playing rugby was really a hobby, despite the fact that I was, much to my surprise, to receive more England trials later. I found coaching immensely rewarding, and the unbeaten Marlborough team of 1956, together with victory in the Rosslyn Park Sevens in 1957, meant a great deal to me. It must have meant something to the boys too, for the Sevens team invited me back to a reunion dinner at Marlborough forty years later.

It was during my first headmastership at Ellesmere College that I first became involved with the Rugby Football Union. A group of us had long felt that the game required coaches and that we ought to be writing a coaching manual, with the idea of eventually setting up a whole series of properly qualified rugby football coaches throughout the country.

I was asked to chair the first ever RFU coaching conference for all constituent bodies at Lilleshall from 29 August to 4 September 1964 to discuss these ideas. As a result of those deliberations I was invited to put together a group of people to write a coaching manual for the RFU. The group consisted of Jeff Butterfield, with whom I had played for England; Bob MacEwen, who had played many times for Scotland and with whom I played at Cambridge University; Ray Williams who was later to become the Secretary of the Welsh Football Union; Howell Griffiths, who had played with me at Cambridge University and was teaching at Uppingham and, finally, as the link with the past, Mark Sugden who played many times for Ireland and had been involved in the only other coaching pamphlet to have been produced by the RFU, before the Second World War.

I chose this group in order to involve experts from all the four countries in the United Kingdom and test out whether the RFU was prepared to be open-minded enough to be influenced by our rivals on the international field. I know that some of the RFU Committee were none too happy but I was not prepared to carry out the task unless I was given a free hand. Permission was granted and we began our work. The final product was called *A Guide for Coaching* and consisted of ten pamphlets in a loose-leaf binder so that it could be up-dated. It was eventually reprinted in various countries around the world, including a version in Japanese.

My love of rugby football stemmed from my days at Whitgift School where I was coached by Freddie Percy and Jack Cummings, two of my schoolteachers. The latter became a headmaster and is no longer alive, but Freddie is as strong and upright today as he was then, having just celebrated his ninetieth birthday. After leaving Whitgift I played in the Army during my national service and then went up to Cambridge where I played in three University matches, captaining the side in 1954.

I remember well travelling from Cambridge on the evening of Monday 8 December for the 1952 University match and arriving at King's Cross station to be faced by the worst smog of the century. We put our bags in the taxi and walked ahead of the driver shining torches onto the curb. Our new pale Blue scarves were moistened and wrapped around our faces as we tried not to breathe in the polluted air. It took us a very long time to walk to the Grosvenor House Hotel in Park Lane where we were staying, and I believe that very few of us felt we would be playing a match at Twickenham the next day. That night hundreds died in London and the Clean Air Act was born. It was the worst, and the last, of the great London smogs.

To our surprise the air had cleared by the next day and we travelled to Twickenham in four Daimler hire cars with police outriders on their motorcycles. We went the wrong way round roundabouts and through traffic lights. It was quite exciting and we felt more important than we should have done. Although the crowd today is almost as big as it was in those days, the game then was more prominently featured in the rugby calendar and was looked upon as a trial for the different home countries with all the selectors present. The preparation of the team was left entirely in the hands of the captain. When I was elected captain for 1954 I decided, together with the secretary, Peter Davies (the son of Emrys Davies of Glamorgan cricket fame) and the treasurer, Bob MacEwen, the Scottish hooker, that we should invite a different prominent international player to watch each of our games. The international player then dined with us after the match and analysed our play critically. We used these players to inspire us to become coaches in our own right. At that time no United Kingdom team had the kind of coach whose presence is taken for granted today.

We experimented with various tactics, with magnetic boards, with films, with as many new ideas as we could muster. Although we beat every side bar one we played that year, we realised that if the other clubs were to organise themselves better and have proper coaches, neither Cambridge nor Oxford University would find winning so easy.

This was the background which inspired us to lead the RFU into the era of coaching.

In 1965 we asked Don Rutherford to act as our eyes and ears when he was on tour playing with the British Lions in New Zealand. He returned with many ideas and the following year joined the Coaching Panel, which I was chairing and which was responsible for advising the RFU. That same year the British Council sent me out to Sri Lanka (then called Ceylon) to coach every rugby team in that country, both school and adult teams. I was very fortunate to be able to carry out such an enterprise during my holidays as headmaster and even more fortunate that I was allowed to take my wife with me. The Rugby Football Union of Sri Lanka was immensely kind to us and, during a break in coaching, I remember watching England win the soccer World Cup of 1966 on television.

Coaching was becoming established in the rugby football world, although many were still very suspicious that it might lead to a professional approach, which in the end of course it did. In 1969 the Rugby Football Union decided they needed someone at Twickenham to lead and direct coaching. It was typical of those days that they could not, or did not wish to, refer to coaching in the job title and so the first Technical Administrator, Don

Rutherford, was appointed from the Coaching Advisory Panel. His great service to coaching throughout the world was recognised in 2001 by the award of the OBE.

In 1972 I was elected by the University of Cambridge to the Committee of the Rugby Football Union under the chairmanship of Dr Tom Kemp, the Cambridge representative. I therefore moved from being Chairman of the Coaching Advisory Panel to being Chairman of the Coaching Subcommittee itself. The subcommittee ran a large number of courses and conferences and a pyramid of coaches was being developed throughout the country. I was however becoming increasingly concerned about the number of injuries within the game and was appointed the first Chairman of the Injuries Prevention Committee. That committee succeeded in having the laws of the game changed to make scrummaging safer. In the eighties the game was creating about ten paraplegics a season. In recent years this number has been reduced to only two or three, still two or three too many.

For most of my time at Lancing, and throughout my time at Harrow, I had to attend rugby meetings, chair coaching courses and conferences as well as attend many dinners and matches without allowing it to affect my professional life. The game was my hobby. It was great to be able to attend all these functions and not to be treated as a headmaster. My colleagues enjoyed pulling the leg of a headmaster just as they had when I had been playing. In those days it was all part of the spirit and fun of the game. We all knew that no one was involved for money. They were in it for the love of the game and for the camaraderie. Only once did my professional life and my hobby overlap and that was during my first year at Harrow. The School XV had not won a game for two years and, after my first year, the situation was no better. I knew we had to find someone from outside who would have the respect of all and change the atmosphere. I persuaded Roger Uttley, the ex-England captain, to give up his work with a remedial back specialist and return to teaching. I knew he would be superb running the rugby, but I wanted him to be in charge of all physical education and knew we would have to build a new physical education centre if we were to keep him. Moreover, although he was a trained teacher, he had no degree and I was concerned about how my colleagues at Harrow would take the appointment of the first ever master not to be a graduate. I need not have worried, as one of my senior academics was praising Roger's personality by the end of his first term, and Roger himself had signed up to study for a masters degree at Brunel. He is now a graduate, has a new Physical Education centre and has been responsible for inspiring three pupils to go on and represent their countries; Gareth Rees, Captain of Canada, Damian Hopley and Fraser Walters of England. These three were in addition to two who were my pupils at Ellesmere: Bill Beaumont and Mark Keyworth, both of whom played for England.

My experience playing for England and Wales against Scotland and Ireland in 1955 when the 'new' stand at Lansdowne Road was opened was typical. We were all in the changing room and Cliff Morgan of Wales was our captain. He took me on one side and asked me to lead the forwards and have a word with them before we went on to the pitch. Cliff took the three-quarters away and I looked at 'my' charges: six Welsh internationals, many with great household names, and only one other Englishman. The great Welsh front row of Bryn Meredith, Stokoe Williams and Courteney Meredith were playing liar dice, totally absorbed. 'Come on chaps, gather round', I said in true Cambridge style. There was a stunned silence and then one of the liar dice players said, fairly forcibly 'F*** O**, Professor!' I decided to join in the liar dice. A little later I said to Cliff Morgan 'OK Cliff, we are ready.' Thank goodness we won.

We retired from Harrow in August 1991 and travelled through the USA from Alaska to Texas lecturing on education before returning to England for the World Cup in the late autumn. There was the World Coaching Congress to Chair and the worries I had over injuries to players were at the forefront of my mind.

I then travelled as Junior Vice President in 1992 with the England second team to watch their matches against Italy, France and Spain. Angela came with me on each occasion, and the players could not have been more welcoming and friendly, especially the captain, Stuart Barnes, now a TV commentator and journalist. I always undertook some light training with the team and together we enjoyed Rome, Paris and Madrid. Angela was welcomed to all the receptions and dinners. Although the only lady present in Rome, she was beautifully hosted by our Italian friends. After their victories in all their international matches in 1992, I travelled to New Zealand to be with them for a while the following year. Jack Rowell was their manager and coach and was to become the coach to the senior side the next season. They were a very fine group of players and great ambassadors for England.

My concerns over injuries in the game, and especially serious neck injuries, made me decide, when I was elected President of the RFU in 1993, to create a new charity called SPIRE (Support Paraplegics in Rugby Enterprise). HRH Prince Edward kindly agreed to head up the charity and inspired me to aim for a far larger capital sum than I had originally intended. I thought that if we raised a half a million pounds we would do well. Prince Edward wanted to raise £2 million so we eventually settled on one million. It is very encouraging that in the 2001 season the capital sum stands at between

£3 million and £4 million with the income going to help support the 104 para-plegics in England. These ex-players are now able to keep in touch with one another and with Twickenham, and are invited, together with their carers, to watch matches there.

In the summer of 1993 the game was at a crossroads. Players were making a lot of money through sponsors, advertising, opening stores and similar activities. There were even rumours that players in the antipodes and South Africa were being paid to play the game, in contravention of the International Board Laws.

It was the express wish of the RFU Committee that no players should be paid for playing the game and I tried to encourage the Union to enter into contracts with the international players. I could envisage, at a later date, players' agents and the senior clubs controlling the players rather than the Union itself. I could not, however, get the support that was needed at that time. It was left that England would do its best, through its two members on the International Board, to resist any move to pay players for playing, and would concentrate on changing the Laws so that players could make as much money as they were able to through sponsorship, advertising and the like. It was felt that the game was not ready for professionalism and too many of the Committee were totally opposed to the idea, myself included. After all, was it not a hobby, a pastime, something from which you did not make money, but rather put money into, so that youngsters could have as much fun as we had had? This was the very essence of the game as it had been instilled in us from a very young age. We were, however, all out of touch with the prevailing wind, coming in the main from the antipodes and South Africa, which was destined to blow us all away.

I wanted to bring the Presidents of the home Unions closer together so that we could discuss some of the problems facing the game and decided to hold a dinner for them all in London. However, I needed an inducement for them to come over to England yet again as they spent so much of their time travelling here; I wondered whether to hold the meeting in another part of the United Kingdom. So I thought long and hard about a good venue; but the difficulty was that we had all dined in the most prestigious venues in London on previous occasions. Suddenly I hit upon the Tower of London. What a wonderful place for the four countries to meet! I wrote to the Governor and he informed me, fairly briskly, that the Tower was not used for that kind of event. However, if I invited them as an erstwhile subaltern of the Royal Fusiliers (City of London Regiment), we could dine in the Fusiliers Officers' Mess in the White Tower. The invitation went out from an erstwhile subaltern who happened, for the moment, to be President of the RFU. All accepted, with the President of the Scottish Union accepting as an erstwhile trooper in the Royal Horse Guards. We had an excellent evening but were all concerned about the direction the game was taking. We were all people brought up in the old amateur tradition of service for no reward.

It is therefore hardly surprising that the unhappiest time of my presidency took place at the end of my year in office when we accompanied the England team to South Africa for the first time since apartheid. It should have been a joyous tour; the team played divine rugby in Pretoria, thrashing South Africa, but came a cropper at Cape Town. It was not joyous because of the deceit that was running through the game. It was being organised and played under the international laws of amateurism but underneath it was professional; the administrators of England and South Africa had totally opposite perceptions of the game and of its future.

Very early on my wife and I were invited to dine with some young old pupils of ours who lived in South Africa. They told us they were paid for playing, and they were not very good players. They told me that all the players received their rands and I felt that this was probably a by-product of apartheid, when no players could be enticed into the country without payment. Whatever the cause, the result appeared to be a total disregard of the laws of the game. I wrote to my opposite number, Dr Louis Luyt, and asked him whether any players were paid and, if so, why. He assured me that he had looked into the matter and found no evidence that any players were being paid for playing in his country.

A few days later we were at another game where Vice President de Klerk was in attendance. He came up to me to ask whether it was true that I had made a speech in Pretoria warning of the dangers of going professional. I told him that I had indeed made such a speech. He asked me, why on earth did I object to paying the players? He said that they paid all their players in South Africa, so why didn't we?

I explained to the Vice President that it was against the laws of the game but then went on to try and explain the philosophical reasons why I felt it was unwise. I had for example met coaches of junior teams in South Africa who thanked me for my amateur stance explaining that they were already suffering as a result of the professionalisation of the game in their country. There had previously been sufficient money to enable them to coach and organise junior rugby teams but, they said, the money was now going to the top players and their position was becoming impossible. In other words, the grass roots of the game were not being nurtured, a situation which, sadly, we are now seeing in our own country and which the RFU has to address.

De Klerk replied by informing me that 'As we pay all our players I simply do not understand why you do not.' I asked him to go and have a word with Dr Louis Luyt and give him this information as he, Luyt, knew of no players in South Africa who were paid!

At a meeting of the International Board in August 1995 the game went professional. The move was led, so I am told, by South Africa and the southern hemisphere and was not opposed by England as strongly as we, and others, had hoped. Despite the fact that it required a two-thirds majority for such a major change in the laws, the decision was taken without a vote. In England the game is still trying to cope with professionalism and, in my view, the grass roots are suffering. Indeed, many of the consequences of the move to professionalism are as I predicted at the AGM of the Union in 1994. Nevertheless the clock cannot be turned back and, on the positive side, England are probably now playing the finest rugby they have ever played. For that we must rejoice, whatever our personal preferences may be.

I immediately resigned from the RFU Committee, as I had always said that I would not turn my hobby into a business and I wanted nothing to do with the administration of the professional game. My letter of resignation is still on file but I was asked not to make it public, as it would not help the RFU, and its then President, in tackling the problem of the future.

Instead, I wrote a paper suggesting that all clubs should have the opportunity to choose whether they wished to go professional or stay amateur. I drew up simple regulations enabling players to switch from amateur to professional status and back again, thus ensuring freedom of movement. I suggested that ten members of the RFU Committee, who were businessmen and wanted to run the professional game, should be put in charge. The Committee would be responsible both for the professional game, through the ten-man subcommittee, but also for the amateur game, so preserving something of the long tradition which had been built up by our predecessors. The scheme was rejected by the working party looking into the professional game, as they believed there could be no such division. In their words, the game had to become 'seamless'.

When I was playing for Cambridge and England, I was taken on one side by the then President of the RFU, Sir William Ramsay, who said to me, 'Ian, you will have a great deal to put back into this game after all that it has given you. I hope you will accept that challenge.' I did accept the challenge and the game became my relaxation and hobby until August 1995 when the modern era began. The irony of my situation was that my enthusiasm for coaching which began in 1954 led to one of the changes which made professionalism inevitable. I just hope and pray that my successors who now run the RFU can manage the new era and somehow maintain the game at school level, including providing good referees. There are many problems but for parents of young men playing the game, I would highlight one in particular.

The tackle, crucial to the game as a body contact sport, is defined clearly in the laws. Nowhere, however, is the purpose of the tackle set out, and the answer to that question is a fertile subject for debate. Is it to deprive the opposition of the ball? Or to do that and make the player less keen to receive it next time? Or to remove the player from the game temporarily or even permanently? The cries of 'the big hit', 'take him out' have replaced the old cry of 'tackle him'. For parents, the change is important and worrying. Unless the game is enjoyable and played for fun, with minimum injuries and good referees, parents and young people may vote with their feet and play one of the many other games on offer which will give them enjoyment and keep them fit with less physical risk.

A lot of thinking is needed if the spirit of a great game is to be kept alive so as to give young people the experience and fun that so many of my generation were privileged to receive. It is now up to others give back to the game something of that which they have themselves received; I just hope that the new professionals will understand what that means.

30

Physical Education and the General Teaching Council

IN my last year at Harrow (1990–1991) I was asked to be the Chairman of the Working Group which created the syllabus for physical education in the new National Curriculum. I was surprised to be asked, but not nearly as surprised as were the members of the Working Group itself. I assumed that I would have a say as to who would sit on this Group but the Secretary of State for Education made it clear to me that I would be chairing the members he had chosen. I was a little concerned whether I would have the time and energy to complete the task, but it was too exciting to refuse.

The Working Group consisted of thirteen members and myself and we were served by a secretariat of six people. We had two assessors, one from the Department of Education and Science and one from Her Majesty's Inspectorate.

The members were a wonderful group of people from a very wide range of backgrounds. The Secretary of State felt that physical education was something to which many lay people could contribute. The Group included the sportsmen, John Fashanu and Steve Ovett, the Education Officer for the Arts Council, a lecturer from Birmingham University Medical School and a Professor of Geography who was an expert on outward bound. There were also a Head and two Deputy Heads, an Education Officer, a manager with IBM and a banker. Finally, we had two Professors of Physical Education from universities, as well as a physical education adviser from a local education authority.

I realised at once that we would have to spend some time bringing the Group together as a unit. At the first meeting there was clearly a language problem. The two professors spoke about physical education using terminology and concepts which quite a few people round the table could not understand. Others approached it from their own perspective and were on occasion just as unintelligible. At the end of the first meeting John Fashanu, for example, was honest enough to say that he had not understood what anybody had said. It was clear that we would have to simplify our approach.

At that meeting I made my first mistake and suggested that the members might like to meet at Harrow School. I fear I made the suggestion selfishly, as I was concerned about the amount of time I might have to spend away from the school. My suggestion fell on stony ground and was refused.

We held our meetings in different places all over the country. We visited countries in Europe. We visited many schools. We watched PE classes and we heard the views of PE teachers. I was on a great learning curve and found the work extremely stimulating.

I had not anticipated that during the period of our work we would have for our master three different Secretaries of State. I recall going to bed early in a hotel in the north of England and being woken by a telephone call from John MacGregor, who was then Secretary of State for Education. I almost stood to attention and wondered what we had done wrong. It turned out that he was simply telephoning to inquire how we were getting on and whether there was anything he could do to help us. Remarkable thoughtfulness from a very busy but incredibly kind man.

I was astonished at the ignorance of politicians concerning sport and physical education. So many of them simply wanted the clock turned back and all children to play soccer, cricket and rugby; hockey, possibly, but even that was regarded by some as a little too 'way out'. When I suggested to one minister that basketball was a fine game, especially for inner-city schools where there might be no playing fields, I was told 'We do not want to turn youngsters into a load of poofters!' I knew, of course, of the work-to-rule strike introduced by my colleagues in the maintained sector which had led to the cancellation of so many sporting fixtures. Their initiative was inspired by the most damaging piece of government legislation I can ever remember being introduced into the educational world. Kenneth Baker, then Secretary of State, was determined to discipline idle teachers and imposed minimum hours of w . This resulted in the vast majority of teachers—to whom precious few thanks were given for hours of unpaid overtime—rebelling. The profession was not being treated as a profession: the action to prevent idle teachers from being lazy may or may not have been necessary, but the way it was introduced was insulting to all teachers. I had young teachers, as well as old, submitting on paper their hours of work, almost double the minimum! When, therefore, Ministers asked me to ensure that the National Curriculum for Physical Education redressed the problem, by re-introducing sporting fixtures and making maintained schools comparable to the independent sector, I had to spend much time trying to explain to them the very deep harm that their earlier decisions had caused. There was no way that a new National Curriculum could solve the problem; it required a fundamentally different approach by politicians to the teaching profession. Theirs was a learning curve, too . . .

We invited one of the ministers (now Sir Robert Atkins) to come to Birmingham to see what we were doing and what some schools could do. He came, was very impressed and his attitude towards physical education was changed from that day on. This was very encouraging but unfortunately we could not do the same for every politician involved. So many wrongly equated physical education with sport. Sport is but one element of physical education, although an important one.

Less encouraging was a meeting I had with the third Secretary of State with whom I worked, Kenneth Clarke. He told us he had learnt that we were planning to make it compulsory for all children in our schools to swim twenty-five metres. He asked me to have this deleted from our plan as the country could not afford it. I was astounded. I replied 'If the country cannot afford it then it must be your responsibility to say so; it is my responsibility to make certain that we insist that in the National Curriculum every child should be taught to swim. It would be monstrous to suggest anything else at all.' I am not at all sure that I pleased him and he was highly critical of much of the work we were doing, but I felt that his view of physical education was extremely narrow. In the event the swimming element in the report was never deleted and remains in the curriculum to this day. I came away from the meeting very cross that the minister had not asked me to thank the Working Group who were, after all, only doing the job for the love of it and had to take time out from their normal professional jobs.

The final report was submitted to the Secretary of State on 28 June 1991 and published in the August, the month I retired from Harrow. The work led to me talking at many conferences held by sporting and physical education organisations, and I was very excited by the thought that all young children would receive a first-class physical education. The maintained sector would then be competing on an equal footing with the independent sector when it came to games and fitness. Indeed, provided the content of our report was implemented, they would probably be given a finer all round physical education. The recommendations, for example, included compulsory dance for younger children. I still maintain that dance at a young age could improve the performance of front row rugby forwards!

It has been a tragedy for me and others to see how over the last ten years so many of our recommendations have been sidelined as other changes have been made in the National Curriculum. I am deeply concerned about the fitness and health of our young people and I worry that during the crucial years of physical development there is too much emphasis on the league tables of academic success. While that academic success is of course crucial, it will be of little use if at the age of forty many of the present generation are suffering from circulatory problems due to a lack of proper exercise during their adolescent years. Success in sport or PE can inspire a young person who is not doing very well academically to have confidence in themselves, and this can lead to vast improvements in the classroom.

Partly I imagine as a consequence of this work, I was asked in February 1992 to become Chairman of the England Sports Council, created alongside the new UK Sports Council, taking up office the following September. I accepted the appointment from John Major, only to find that it had been 'put on ice' because of the Spring General Election. On his re-election I was again invited to take up the post and I accepted. The start of our work was further delayed to January 1993, then to April and then to October, when it was finally abandoned by Peter Brooke, then Secretary of State for National Heritage. I had become totally disillusioned with the government and refused to accept another invitation in October 1993 when Peter Brooke was creating another scheme. I was not sorry, as I found sporting politics frustrating, time consuming and not very interesting.

Whatever criticisms may have come our way, Kenneth Clarke was kind enough, when we had completed our work, to give a dinner party at Lancaster House for the whole of the Working Group to say thank you for all the work we had done. The diverse group had certainly come together and we had our own reunion in the Professor of Geography's house down in the West Country a few years later. And, just to please me, the Working Group voted unanimously that the final meeting should be held at Harrow. I hosted an excellent dinner in the dining room which my predecessor had created; I was silently thanking him once more. Any barriers which may have existed between maintained and independent schools had been broken down. Members told me that they very nearly did not join the Working Group because the Head Master of Harrow was the Chairman and they felt this was the wrong image for the National Curriculum. I fully understood this and it was generous of them to confess to their initial reservations but then emphasise that there really need not have been any doubts at all. It was a happy and constructive conclusion from my point of view.

My final educational role has been to Chair the Independent Schools Council at a time when it became very clear that greater unity was required between all the different Associations that exist within the independent schools. The first Association to be founded was the Head Masters' Conference in 1869, followed by the Independent Schools Association in 1879 and the Incorporated Association of Preparatory Schools in 1892. They were followed, in the twentieth century, by the Girls' Schools Association and the Society of Headmasters and Headmistresses of Independent Schools. These six associations represent the heads of all the independent schools. The bursars then formed their own Bursars' Association, as did the governors, who created the Governing Bodies Association and the Governing Bodies Association of Girls' Schools. The Council, therefore, consists of these eight associations together with our media arm, the Independent Schools Council Information Service.

One of the major tasks of the Council is to liaise with the government of the day and it became very apparent when I became Chairman in 1996 that it was essential for the Department of Education and Employment to be dealing with one body in the independent sector rather than eight. We immediately began an exercise in unity and meetings with Ministers and government officials became part of our regular routine. From this important exercise was born the Independent Schools Inspectorate, the Independent Schools Induction Service for new teachers, schemes for the recruitment of new teachers, in conjunction with the Teacher Training Agency, and so on. Partnership with the Blair government has developed in a creative and purposeful way never previously experienced with any other government since I began teaching in 1955. Whilst retaining our independence, which is the reason for our very existence, we have been able to get closer to our colleagues in the maintained sector, to understand better their problems and to help wherever possible. In carrying out this policy we, too, have learnt a very great deal.

When I retired as Chairman of the Independent Schools Council the school insurers, Holmwoods, very generously gave Angela and me a dinner to say thank you for the voluntary work we had done for independent education. The dinner was held in the board room of their parent company, HSBC. There were forty guests representing all aspects of the independent sector, as well as a few of the politicians with whom I had worked. By a coincidence, the dinner was held the day after Estelle Morris had been appointed Secretary of State for Education. I knew she had been invited in her capacity as Minister of State, but no one expected that on her first day in office as Secretary of State she would be able to attend. To our delight however, we found that not only was the Rt Hon John MacGregor, ex Secretary of State for Education in a previous Conservative government present, but also Baroness Janet Young who had been a Conservative Minister of State, as well

as Lord Butler the recently retired Cabinet Secretary, all, of course, wonderfully supported by their spouses. Finally, Estelle walked in saying that she
could not possibly have missed the evening! For me it was a wonderful occasion; I witnessed a group of us discussing education for all the right reasons
with party politics never mentioned. The fact that we had brought together
all these people of very different political views simply because of education
gave me enormous pleasure. It was a small piece of history as far as independent education was concerned.

The new General Teaching Council was set up by the government in
2000. I found myself representing independent teachers amongst a body of
sixty-four people, all of whom welcomed me in a way that I really do not
believe would have been possible back in 1955 when I entered the profession.
I recalled the maintained secondary modern school in which I taught briefly
and was 'warned off' for continuing to teach after the school day had
finished. I ignored the warning and left the school for the independent sector. I remembered that woodwork, metalwork and peripatetic music teachers were not allowed into the Common Room. I recalled the master who
told me, after a year in the school, that he thought I was 'all right' and that I
could now call him Jennings! It had previously been 'Sir', nothing less. And
now, here I was, with everyone on immediate first name terms and all determined to raise the profile and the standards of the profession.

At the inauguration party of the General Teaching Council the youngest
member of the Council, Usha Devi, spoke of her aspirations for the future. I
followed her, as the oldest member, expressing my delight that a government had, at last, trusted teachers enough to give them the means to control
their own profession. I had always wanted a GTC, as had so many other
teachers. I had written to successive Prime Ministers but had always been
politely turned down for a whole variety of reasons. Now a young person
can join one of the finest of professions, knowing that he or she can help set
the standards, help raise the status of teachers in the eyes of the general
public, and advise and influence successive governments over educational
practice of one kind or another.

I am sometimes asked which of the four schools I served was the best. It is
an inappropriate question as each was best for individual pupils. The secret is
to choose the appropriate school for the talents and aptitudes of the specific
child. Throughout the three decades I headmastered the society from which
the children came altered and evolved yet each school continued to do its
best to teach eternal truths to each child—respect for others, honesty,
compassion, integrity, enthusiasm and so on. Looking back I am not sure the
pupils altered very much, but their parents did, as did the society in which

they lived, and those changes did not make it easier for the schools or for the children growing up with them. So often parents lowered their own standards and yet expected their children not to reflect this. Tension was often created as the schools were not prepared to give way on matters of principle. Early on in my career at one school, I gated the whole school at exeat weekend as I had discovered shop lifting was taking place in the locality. Some of the parents were furious and, insisting that their child or children were honest, demanded to take them out. I refused. It was a difficult time. Eventually parents—the very same ones who had objected so strongly—said how wonderful it was that the school was setting standards. I know that today it is even more difficult for heads, especially in the boarding schools. Occasionally I was as critical of parents as they were of me, but overall they were tremendously supportive of the school to which they had entrusted the education of their children, and I thank them sincerely for that. It meant a great deal to all my colleagues and me as well as to the children themselves.

I am forever grateful to all the teachers and the non-teaching staff who worked with me and for all they achieved for each individual child. Their dedication and total involvement in the schools I led so often kept me going at difficult times.

I am also forever grateful to pupils who took responsibility and showed care and compassion for those younger than them and grateful as well to those who were naughty and rebellious so keeping me constantly 'on my toes'! All were a real encouragement to me and made the whole job worthwhile. They were as brilliant in the fifties as they were in the eighties as developing human nature does not alter very much whatever unfair pressures we may inflict on the young.

In many ways I wish I were now starting again. At least I would know something of the pitfalls after all the mistakes I have made over the past forty-five years. I had the privilege of serving four wonderful schools, working with dedicated men and women and making the acquaintance of (and sometimes friends with) with about four thousand stimulating young people.

My mind goes back to my first appointment at Marlborough. I was travelling by train from Bexhill-on-Sea to London, where I lived with my parents, to start my first term down in Wiltshire. My companion was my father, who was working at Lloyds Register of Shipping as Chief Statistician. I said to him on the journey, 'I don't know why you travel to London every day of your life. Why did you not do something really exciting and become a schoolteacher?' I was stunned by the reply. 'All my life', he said, 'I wanted to be a teacher but I was never given the chance.' My parents did give me the chance and I thank them with all my heart.